Healing from Abuse: Authentic Hope Women's Support Group Manual

Door of Hope Ministries

Door of Hope Ministries

Healing from Abuse: Authentic Hope Women's Support Group Manual

Copyright © 2019 by Door of Hope Ministries
All rights reserved. This book or any portion thereof
may not be reproduced or used in any manner whatsoever
without the express written permission of the publisher
except for the use of brief quotations in a book review.

All Scripture quotations, unless otherwise indicated, are taken
from the Holy Bible, New International Version®, NIV®.
Copyright ©1973, 1978, 1984, 2011 by Biblica, Inc.™
Used by permission of Zondervan. All rights reserved worldwide.
www.zondervan.com The "NIV" and "New International Version"
are trademarks registered in the United States Patent and
Trademark Office by Biblica, Inc.™

Scripture quotations marked (NLT) are taken from the Holy Bible,
New Living Translation, copyright ©1996, 2004, 2015
by Tyndale House Foundation. Used by permission of
Tyndale House Publishers, Inc., Carol Stream, Illinois 60188.
All rights reserved.

Printed in the United States of America

First Printing, 2019

Door of Hope Ministries
PO Box 490565
Blaine, MN 55449
Phone 763-767-2150
Email info@doorofhopeministries.org
www.doorofhopeministries.org

ISBN: 9781086856217

> To access additional resources, visit
> doorofhopeministries.org/resources

Healing from Abuse: Authentic Hope Women's Support Group

Table of Contents

About Door of Hope Ministries 1

    Meet Founder and Global Director, Diane Stores 1

    Diane's Message to You 2

Boundaries and Guidelines 3

Eight Steps to Recovery 5

Step One: Recognize Your Powerlessness 7

    Step One Homework & Journaling 15

Step Two: Created for Wholeness 17

    Step Two Homework & Journaling 29

Step Three: God's Plan for Me 31

    Step Three Homework & Journaling 41

Step Four: I am God's Child and I am Being Renewed in His Image 43

    Remember Who You Are 48

    Step Four Homework & Journaling 51

Step Five: Identify What I Need to Take Responsibility For 53

    Step Five Homework & Journaling 57

Step Six: Share My Feelings with Others 59

    Step Six Homework & Journaling 63

Step Seven: Forgiveness 65

    Step Seven Homework & Journaling 69

Step Eight: Developing Healthy Relationships 71

    Step Eight Homework & Journaling 81

Recommended Resources 83

Healing from Abuse: Authentic Hope Support Group *Evaluation Form* 85

About Door of Hope Ministries

Acting locally and globally, Door of Hope Ministries is bringing God's healing from trauma and abuse to the peoples of the world.

Our Mission: Through God's power, Door of Hope equips people all over the world to live free from abuse and trauma through safe housing, educational conferences, support groups, trauma recovery counseling and prayer ministry.

Our Key Verse: There I will give back her vineyards to her and transform her Valley of Troubles into a Door of Hope. - Hosea 2:15a (Living Bible)

Meet Founder and Global Director, Diane Stores

Diane Stores, Founder and Global Director

In 1991, Door of Hope Founder and Global Director, Diane Stores, lived with her husband and children on the west coast.

For 23 years, she had endured abuse at the hands of her husband. Desperate for a way out, she secretly packed the kids into their car and escaped to Minnesota, where her parents lived.

She arrived in Minnesota with an empty tank, $1 in her pocket, and "God, please help me!" in her heart.

Upon arrival, God provided her a job and a home for her family, giving her immense hope for their future. The pain and shame, though, did not go away, so she looked for faith-based help that would counsel her and her children. In those days there were no Christian organizations to help...and the secular sector only had a few 30-day shelters with little more than housing to offer.

Although times were hard...

God used those days to plant a seed in Diane's heart...

Once she became independent and strong enough spiritually and emotionally, Diane set out to help other women needing support. In 1998 she founded one of the first Christian domestic abuse shelters in the United States. And in 2014 she founded Door of Hope, with the vision to minister globally to those affected by abuse and trauma.

Door of Hope has served more than 1,000 men, women, teens and children through support groups, classes, counseling, and leadership training. We've also reached hundreds more through conferences and workshops.

> *Having a safe place for me AND my son to learn about who we are in Christ, what to do with pain, how to process our emotions, how to trust, and how to heal through the Love of the Father, has been vital for our spiritual, emotional, and mental health. I am forever grateful for Door of Hope. - Veronica S.*

We know Jesus is not done, though, as the Prince of Peace is directing us to reach more so that He can answer the prayers of the child in Mexico, the woman in India, the man in Ireland, the teen in China...

We pray that God will use this manual to help fulfill that vision.

Today, Diane's family is a living testament to the healing God brings to generations when one person steps out in faith for their family.

We see it every day at Door of Hope: ***Through God's love and power, families can be transformed for generations, bringing His love and peace to communities, nations and the world.***

Diane's Message to You

Hello Dear Friends,

I'm so excited you've chosen to start this healing journey. This is often one of the hardest things you'll ever do but one of the most worthwhile. I personally understand the courage and strength it takes to begin this process. I applaud your brave heart in taking this step!

The tools and information you'll find in this manual come from my own life experience. These tools literally brought me out of the depths of pain and discouragement to a place of hope and wholeness. I pray they do the same for you!

My heart is with you as you begin this life-changing journey. May God cover you with His grace and give you His joy and an awareness of His ever-present presence. He truly is our Immanuel!

With much love,

Diane Stores
Global Director
Door of Hope

Support Group

Boundaries and Guidelines

This is your support group. We ask that you commit to the following behaviors. We will ask the other support group members to do the same.

I agree to:

1. **Maintain confidentiality**
   - Don't talk about anything you hear in the group to people outside of the group. Everything said in group is confidential.
   - If all group members do this, the group will develop an atmosphere of trust and openness. Healing is based on trust.

2. **Practice listening**
   - Listen actively and constructively. Listen with acceptance and positive interest.
   - Hear each other out and focus on understanding each one's situation and their feelings.
   - Allow each person (including you) to feel and express their whole range of emotions (pain, grief, anger, joy, confidence, peace).

3. **Choose to participate**
   - There is no requirement to talk or share in the group, but each person is encouraged to. Share in the "I" form. Share from the heart. Talk about how something made you feel.
   - Recognize openness involves risk taking. By taking risks, you discover who you are and what you're capable of becoming. Be as honest as possible in all things.
   - When others are talking, please let them finish without interrupting them.
   - In this group, you're encouraged to share your experiences and your hope in Christ.
   - Give yourself permission to express your thoughts and feelings in this safe atmosphere.

4. **Be sensitive**
   - Some people are outgoing and comfortable sharing feelings, for others this is a new experience. Please avoid dominating the group.
   - Keep your sharing time short, to leave room for all to share.
   - Build up each person and learn to accept support from others. Focus on the positives.

5. **Be well mannered**
    - Refrain from interrupting others when they are sharing and/or responding to their information.
    - When it is your turn to share, focus on sharing about your own feelings and experiences instead of reacting to what other people have shared.

6. **Give advice only when asked for**
    - We will all benefit from each other's stories, and many will find it helpful to process thoughts and feelings aloud.
    - Avoid giving advice or judging. Please offer advice only when it's asked for.
    - We are here to listen, support, and be supported. We are not here to fix, rescue or caretake each other. Each person will be given the opportunity to walk through their pain.
    - It is important that we each take responsibility for working on our own healing.

7. **Recognize healing is done by the power of the Holy Spirit**
    - Allow the Lord to work in the life of each person. There are no pat answers.
    - See yourself, and others in the group, as children of God who are pressing in for healing and freedom.
    - Share what God is doing for you in this process. Your testimony will go far to encourage and give hope to others.
    - Begin to practice recognizing when you're being emotionally triggered by others' stories. Pay attention to these areas, as they are indications that God is showing you an area where He wants to bring truth and healing.

8. **Respect time and attendance**:
    - Please honor start and end times. Being late or absent takes away from the group experience.
    - If what you share doesn't support your recovery, there is no reason to share it. Conversations not directly affecting your recovery, or relating to the group talk, should be shared at break time.
    - Know choosing health can be hard and painful. Make a commitment to stay in the process for as long as it takes.
    - Refrain from trying to explain the situation in detail. Instead, focus on identifying and expressing your feelings about what happened.
    - When going through the questions, please limit sharing time to no more than three minutes per person.

Remember: The enemy does not want you to attend these groups, be on time, or see you experience freedom. Don't be surprised by opposition from the enemy.

Name _____ ***Date*** _____

Eight Steps to Recovery

1. I recognize that I am powerless to heal from abuse, and I look to God for the power to make me whole.

2. I will begin to recognize that God's plan and design for me is to grow in JOY and to be relationally connected to Him and to others.

3. I will begin to explore God's plan for a better life. This life does not include physical, emotional, mental, spiritual, or sexual abuse.

4. I am willing to see myself as a spiritual being, a special child of God who can learn to love, respect, and care for myself.
I recognize the need to identify negative attitudes, defense mechanisms, and feelings connected to my abuse.

5. I will identify areas where I need to take responsibility. The person who abused me is responsible for the abusive acts committed against me. I will not accept the guilt and shame resulting from those acts.

6. I will practice trusting others by sharing my feelings, including anger, fear, sadness, and joy.

7. I will learn to forgive myself, God, and others, and let go of self-destructive behaviors that have held me captive.

8. I will develop positive relationships with God and others by learning appropriate boundaries and the skills necessary for healthy relationships.
I will take steps to continue my healing by changing unhealthy behaviors, growing in relationships, and developing a positive support system in my church and in my community.

Isaiah 61

[1] The Spirit of the Sovereign Lord is upon me,
   for the Lord has anointed me
   to bring good news to the poor.
He has sent me to comfort the brokenhearted
   and to proclaim that captives will be released
   and prisoners will be freed.
[2] He has sent me to tell those who mourn
   that the time of the Lord's favor has come,
   and with it, the day of God's anger against their enemies.
[3] To all who mourn in Israel,
   he will give a crown of beauty for ashes,
a joyous blessing instead of mourning,
   festive praise instead of despair.
In their righteousness, they will be like great oaks
   that the Lord has planted for his own glory. (NLT)

Reflection for a New Beginning

There are things in your soul that God wants to remove far from you. Things like shame, rejection, self-contempt, and fear. There are places in your soul that God wants to heal, truly heal, so you'll know freedom you've not known before. There are burdens that weigh heavy that aren't yours to carry. Jesus wants to hold those for you.

 As you venture into this new year [beginning], may you slow your pace and turn your face towards the One who holds the universe in His hand and who holds you, very close to His heart. You can trust Him. May His deep, restorative work surprise and bless you beyond your wildest dreams. You are priceless to Him. Believe it.[1]

---

[1] Larson, Susie (2019, January 7). *Daily Blessing*. Retrieved from www.susielarson.com. Used with permission.

Step One: Recognize Your Powerlessness

**Step One: I recognize that I am powerless to heal from abuse,
and I look to God for the power to make me whole.**

Psalm 9:10 *The Lord is a refuge for the oppressed, a stronghold in times of trouble. Those who know your Name will trust in You, for You, Lord, have never forsaken those who seek You.*

Isaiah 41:20 *So that people may see and know, may consider and understand, that the hand of the Lord has done this, that the Holy One of Israel has created it.*

Welcome

You're probably here because you've been hurt and betrayed. You may be tired, frightened, frustrated, isolated, angry, sad, depressed, and miserable. It may seem as if there's no way out, and that the chaotic world you live in will go on forever and ever.

But you're also here because you want to heal and to be whole again. You want something different in your life. You're here because you know there's a higher truth than the one you've been living. Inside, something tells you that you deserve better than what you've been experiencing.

Pain has been a big issue. Like all of us, you have avoided pain, and used coping mechanisms to hide your pain.

Coping with Abuse

Examples of coping mechanisms include:

- You live incongruently – smiling on the outside, crying on the inside.
- Denial has become a safe place. Pretending something didn't happen gets easier and easier over time.
- You easily excuse the behavior of others and make excuses for their inappropriate behavior. This can feel easier than setting healthy boundaries or acknowledging your pain.
- You rationalize the behavior of others. "They didn't really mean it." "If only I wouldn't have made them angry."
- You isolate, so no one can get close enough to see what's really going on.
- You blame yourself. You work harder to make things perfect. You become hyper-vigilant, good at controlling your environment to keep yourself and everyone else safe.

Coping mechanisms have felt like lifesavers to you. You have used them to survive, which may have been necessary for a season. But now you realize they have become crutches to keep you from the truth; they have rendered you dysfunctional. You've reached a point where you now say, "No more!"

Pain

God has given you pain to let you know that something is wrong, or that something is happening that isn't good for you. To overcome pain, you must walk in the direction of the pain, not because you like the pain, but because you're determined to find truth and a better and healthier way to live.

You are ready to surrender to God and to trust Him to take your broken heart and transform it into something beautiful. You realize that you are powerless and ready to surrender to the One who is all powerful.

Powerlessness

Definition of "powerlessness":

- To have no strength.
- To have no resources.
- Being unable to do it.
- Lacking the capacity to act.

Recognizing powerlessness, the inability to become whole through self-effort, is the first step to recovery and wholeness. Those who have experienced abuse, have experienced powerlessness. **Being powerless feels very out of control, and many of us try to compensate by trying to be perfect, working harder than anyone else, minimizing the abuse, numbing out, or becoming controlling ourselves.** As it turns out, these behaviors keep us from hearing God and receiving God's true healing.

**Discuss: Which of these responses can you see in your own life?

> *For many years I tried to keep my world in control and to get everything right. I worked hard to keep my outside world from falling apart, even though inside I was devastated and in pieces.*
>
> *When I finally realized that I couldn't do it, that nothing helped, I came to the end of myself. I knew in my own strength I was powerless. This is exactly where God wants us.*
>
> ***I prayed: "God, I don't know what I need, and I don't know when I need it, but today I make the decision to put myself into your hands. I give you permission to do what you want, when you want, in my life."***
>
> *This is a prayer I needed to pray often.*
>
> -Diane Stores, Founder of Door of Hope

**Discuss: What are your responses to the following statements?

What I can control: _____

What I can't control: _____

Powerlessness is powerful. It's an important and necessary starting point on your spiritual journey. It opens a way for you to connect to real power - God.

It is within the context of your relationship with the True and Living Lord Jesus Christ that real healing comes, sanity is restored, and the crooked places in your life are made straight. When you no longer try to get God to do something for you, you allow God to work through you.

The Enemy's Lies

There are two areas the enemy tries to distort: the truth about who God says He is, and the truth about who God says you are.

Abuse often leaves you stripped of your self-worth and blind to how God sees you. You've probably done a lot of pretending to escape reality, and, to survive, have shut down in many ways and believed many lies planted by the enemy.

Lies about You

Some of your pain is from believing things about yourself that are not true. These lies tell you that you're worthless, bad, ugly, incompetent, and unlovable.

Abuse slowly steals your soul, your peace, and your identity. You have not only forgotten who you are (if you ever knew), but you have unknowingly been unable to hear what God is saying to you.

Lies about God

To keep safe, you have built walls around your heart. Walls not only keep bad things out, they keep good things out. Because of the abuse, you may have a distorted image of God, that leads you to mistrust Him. You may see Him as impossible to please, manipulative, cruel, judgmental, out to get you, and likely to leave you.

God sees your distorted views and will be patient and gentle with you as you replace the lies with His truth. He knows what you can handle, and when you are ready to face each part of your abuse and trauma. He'll never be in a hurry with you.

The enemy, and the abusive people in your life, have taken away your choices and pushed you into doing things you didn't want to do. God, however, gently invites you into relationship with Him. He will always give you a choice.

4 Basic Needs in Relationships

1. The first thing you need in any healthy relationship is to feel safe.
2. If you feel safe, you will be open to receiving love from that person.
3. As the relationship progresses you will begin to see your true identity.
4. As your identity becomes clearer, you will begin to discover your purpose.

This is especially true in our relationship with God as our Heavenly Father.

Steps of a Healthy Relationship:

Trust should never be blindly given away. Trust needs to be earned by the person asking for it. So often we meet someone and give them 100% of our trust. This seems to be especially true with male and female relationships, but it can happen with any relationship.

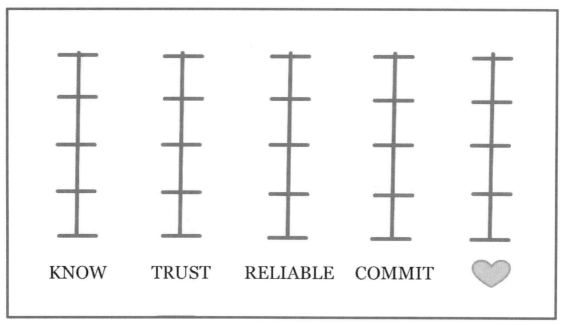

Know – Do you really know them? Have you taken the time to see them in varying situations to see how they act? How do they treat their family and friends? What is the spiritual fruit in their life?

Trust – Do they prove themselves trustworthy? Do they keep things confidential? Do they treasure your vulnerability, or do they use it against you later?

Reliable – Do they honor their commitments to you, to their family and friends, and to their employer? Are they honest in other situations?

Commit – Are they faithful to those they are close to? What does their past pattern of commitment look like? It is often said that the greatest predictor of future behavior is past behavior.

Heart – Until you have walked through these steps with someone – don't give your heart away. Proverbs 4:23 instructs, "Above all else, guard your heart."

Here are some sayings to keep in mind:
- Trust is earned, respect is given, and loyalty is demonstrated. Betrayal of any one of these is to lose all three.
- No one ever gets tired of loving. They get tired of waiting, apologizing, getting disappointed, and being hurt.
- A relationship without trust is like a car without gas; you can stay in it all you want, but it won't go anywhere.

Three Voices

All of us hear three voices: God's voice, the enemy's voice, and our own voice.

God's voice may speak to you about your behavior, but He will never shame you, or put down who you are. The enemy will always attack who you are. Here's a guide to help you determine who is speaking to you:

- **God's voice** – stills you, leads you, reassures you, encourages you, enlightens you, comforts you, calms you, and gently convicts you.
- **The enemy's voice** – rushes you, pushes you, frightens you, confuses you, discourages you, worries you, obsesses you, and condemns you.
- **Your own voice**—our inner voice will choose to agree with either God's voice or the enemy's voice. It is important for us to be aware of that and choose to believe God's truth, rather than the enemy's lies.

God loves your questions. When you hear something and you are not sure who is speaking, just ask Him:

- "Lord, is this you?"
- "Lord, what do you want me know?"
- "Lord, how do you see me?"

He will be faithful in teaching you to follow His voice. He promises you in John 10:27, *"My sheep hear My voice."*

What to expect as you journey into healing

During this support group, you will explore what God says about you. You will look at His Word and find the truth about who He has created you to be. You will shed the lies that the enemy, and others, have said about you. Rather than using your energy to survive, you will focus your energy on healing.

You will look at your misconceptions of God. As you risk letting Him in, little by little, the Holy Spirit will begin to melt away your protective walls so you can let God's love in. You will begin to see Him as He really is.

It's very helpful to know how trauma affects our brains. The next section will show us how abuse and pain have affected our brain and, ultimately, our reactions to all of life's situations.

Psalm 18: God's response when you're hurt

Psalm 18 describes how God responds when His child is being hurt.

This Psalm is part of your homework. Put yourself in this Psalm.

- Verse 2: Declare that God is your fortress and your deliverer.
- Verse 4: You feel the cords of death tangled around you.
- Verse 6: You cry out to God in your distress, and see that God hears you! He hears your cries! He not only hears, but He responds with anger. The mountains begin to shake.
- Verse 8: You see smoke coming from His nostrils and fire coming from His mouth.
- Verse 9: He parts the heavens and comes down to rescue you. What an amazing reaction to His child, to you!

As Psalm 18 goes on, He shoots His arrows and scatters the enemies coming against you. Then, our sweet and amazing God reaches down and gently takes hold of you, pulling you out of that dark place, saving you from the ones who were too strong for you.

- Psalm 18:19: This is a beautiful statement of our Father's heart for us:
  "I rescued you because I delighted in you!"
- Then He heals you, trains you, and arms you to fight the enemy in His strength.
- This is the journey you are on! This is the path He has chosen for you.

During group time, we'll explore more of His wonderful truth. He's with you and He's for you. If you don't retreat, He will give you victory.

Psalm 18 – From Victim to Victor

¹ I love you, Lord, my strength.

² The Lord is my rock, my fortress and my deliverer;
  my God is my rock, in whom I take refuge,
  my shield and the horn of my salvation, my stronghold.

³ I called to the Lord, who is worthy of praise,
  and I have been saved from my enemies.

⁴ The cords of death entangled me;
  the torrents of destruction overwhelmed me.

⁵ The cords of the grave coiled around me;
  the snares of death confronted me.

⁶ In my distress I called to the Lord;
  I cried to my God for help.
From his temple he heard my voice;
  my cry came before him, into his ears.

⁷ The earth trembled and quaked,
  and the foundations of the mountains shook;
  they trembled because he was angry.

⁸ Smoke rose from his nostrils;
  consuming fire came from his mouth,
  burning coals blazed out of it.

⁹ He parted the heavens and came down;
  dark clouds were under his feet.

¹⁰ He mounted the cherubim and flew;
  he soared on the wings of the wind.

¹¹ He made darkness his covering, his canopy around him—
  the dark rain clouds of the sky.

¹² Out of the brightness of his presence clouds advanced,
  with hailstones and bolts of lightning.

¹³ The Lord thundered from heaven;
  the voice of the Most High resounded.

¹⁴ He shot his arrows and scattered the enemy,
  with great bolts of lightning he routed them.

¹⁵ The valleys of the sea were exposed
  and the foundations of the earth laid bare
at your rebuke, Lord,
  at the blast of breath from your nostrils.

¹⁶ He reached down from on high and took hold of me;
  he drew me out of deep waters.

¹⁷ He rescued me from my powerful enemy,
  from my foes, who were too strong for me.

¹⁸ They confronted me in the day of my disaster,
  but the Lord was my support.

¹⁹ He brought me out into a spacious place;
  he rescued me because he delighted in me.

²⁰ The Lord has dealt with me according to my righteousness;
  according to the cleanness of my hands he has rewarded me.

²¹ For I have kept the ways of the Lord;
  I am not guilty of turning from my God.

²² All his laws are before me;
  I have not turned away from his decrees.

²³ I have been blameless before him
  and have kept myself from sin.

²⁴ The Lord has rewarded me according to my righteousness,
  according to the cleanness of my hands in his sight.

²⁵ To the faithful you show yourself faithful,
  to the blameless you show yourself blameless,

²⁶ to the pure you show yourself pure,

but to the devious you show yourself shrewd.

²⁷ You save the humble
　but bring low those whose eyes are haughty.
²⁸ You, Lord, keep my lamp burning;
　my God turns my darkness into light.
²⁹ With your help I can advance against a troop;
　with my God I can scale a wall.

³⁰ As for God, his way is perfect:
　The Lord's word is flawless;
　he shields all who take refuge in him.
³¹ For who is God besides the Lord?
　And who is the Rock except our God?

³² It is God who arms me with strength
　and keeps my way secure.
³³ He makes my feet like the feet of a deer;
　he causes me to stand on the heights.
³⁴ He trains my hands for battle;
　my arms can bend a bow of bronze.
³⁵ You make your saving help my shield,
　and your right hand sustains me;
　your help has made me great.
³⁶ You provide a broad path for my feet,
　so that my ankles do not give way.

³⁷ I pursued my enemies and overtook them;
　I did not turn back till they were destroyed.
³⁸ I crushed them so that they could not rise;
　they fell beneath my feet.
³⁹ You armed me with strength for battle;
　you humbled my adversaries before me.
⁴⁰ You made my enemies turn their backs in flight,
　and I destroyed my foes.

⁴¹ They cried for help, but there was no one to save them—
　to the Lord, but he did not answer.
⁴² I beat them as fine as windblown dust;
　I trampled them like mud in the streets.
⁴³ You have delivered me from the attacks of the people;
　you have made me the head of nations.
People I did not know now serve me,
⁴⁴ 　foreigners cower before me;
　as soon as they hear of me, they obey me.
⁴⁵ They all lose heart;
　they come trembling from their strongholds.

⁴⁶ The Lord lives! Praise be to my Rock!
　Exalted be God my Savior!
⁴⁷ He is the God who avenges me,
　who subdues nations under me,
⁴⁸ 　who saves me from my enemies.
You exalted me above my foes;
　from a violent man you rescued me.
⁴⁹ Therefore I will praise you, Lord, among the nations;
　I will sing the praises of your name.

⁵⁰ He gives his king great victories;
　he shows unfailing love to his anointed,
　to David and to his descendants forever.

Step One
Homework & Journaling

Step One: I recognize that I am powerless to heal from abuse, and I look to God for the power to make me whole.

1. What does the word "power" mean to me? Is it positive or negative?

2. Who are some of the "powerful" and/or controlling people in my life?

3. How do I feel in those situations?

4. What is the difference between the powerlessness in an unhealthy or abusive relationship, and being powerless before God?

5. Do I believe God has the power to make me whole? Why or why not?

6. What some are key things/goals you would like to see God do in your life in the next eight weeks?

7. Read through Psalm 18 and highlight the parts of this Psalm that have special meaning to you.

Step Two: Created for Wholeness

Step Two: I will begin to recognize that God's plan and design for me is to grow in JOY and to be relationally connected to Him and to others.

Nehemiah 8:10 *The Joy of the Lord is my strength.*

Psalm 91:15 *When they call on me, I will answer; I will be with them in trouble. I will rescue and honor them.*

Jeremiah 33:3 *Ask me and I will tell you remarkable secrets you do not know about things to come.*

Isaiah 40:31 *But those who trust [or hope] in the LORD will find new strength. They will soar high on wings like eagles. They will run and not grow weary. They will walk and not faint.*

In this lesson we are going to study how trauma affects the brain and how to return to joy and connection with God and others, as we find wholeness through God's power and grace.

Our Brains are Designed for Spirituality

- Brain research has shown that faith and spiritual practices can have a dramatic effect on the quality of your life.
- Healthy faith and spiritual practices can decrease alcohol use, depression, suicide, divorce, and stress. They can also increase happiness, wellbeing, sexual satisfaction within marriage, and longevity.
- **If we believe God is an authoritative, punishing "god," scientists have discovered that this can negatively affect our brain and body by...**
    - Inflaming the brain's fear center.
    - Shrinking the brain.
    - Damaging the brain's pre-frontal cortex.
    - Impairing the brain's healing and growth.
    - Increasing stress hormones.
    - Increasing blood pressure and heart rate.
    - Damaging the brain and causing early death.
- **However, if we believe God is a Loving God, we experience positive effects, such as:**
    - Sharpened thinking and improved memory.
    - Our brain is stimulated to heal and grow.
    - Reduced religious anxiety, guilt, fear, and anger.
    - Decreased negative activity in our amygdala (the brain's fear center).
    - The walls and unhealthy boundaries between us and God can be dissolved.
    - Healthier brains and more "happy chemicals" released into our systems.
    - Feelings of being bonded, connected and loved by God, and others.
    - Hope arises. Hope changes the circuits in our brain, so we don't default to one of the Three Fs of Fear: Fight, Flee or Freeze.

Effects of Trauma on the Brain

Within the last forty years, science has discovered that the left and right hemispheres of the brain have unique and specific functions. Research generally identifies the left brain as the academic brain and the right brain as the artistic brain. Studies conclude that learning increases at astounding rates when students integrate both sides of their brain during a lesson.

This diagram illustrates left brain and right brain functions. The brain splits up functioning, and then coordinates and synchronizes information processing between the two halves. When a person has received appropriate healthy bonding at an early age, the left and right brain work in harmony to regulate emotion and process information.

When trauma happens at an early age, disconnect happens. When there is a disconnect between the two halves, the right brain shuts down in stressful situations and is unable to access what the left brain knows.

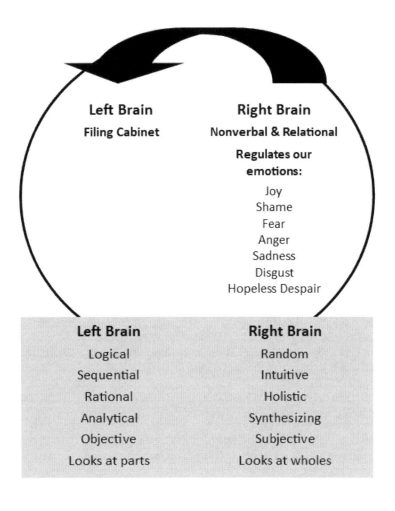

When our control center is functioning <u>the way God created it</u>, our right brain connects to our left brain so we can access what we know to be true.

Trauma A and Trauma B

(From *Living From The Heart Jesus Gave You*[2])

People seem to understand that when it comes to medical problems, that a correct diagnosis is necessary. It is no different when it comes to trauma recovery. To recover, we must first properly and thoroughly identify the wounds.

Traumas can usually be divided into two categories: Type A trauma and Type B trauma.

Type A trauma comes from the lack of good things we should all receive, things that give us emotional stability.

- **These absences create difficulties in relationships**. Painful feelings surface when a person begins to realize the things they have missed.
- The areas of the brain most seriously affected by Type A traumas are the places where strong emotions are handled.
- Since the soul is primarily devoted to emotions, **we can call Type A trauma fractures of the soul.**
- **Type A recovery requires enduring love relationships** to overcome negative emotions. Letting deep feelings emerge and developing trust are needed to cultivate enough strength to face painful feelings. This takes time, and it takes the presence of real loving relationships.

Oftentimes, Type A traumas are given little attention. Their importance can be denied, leaving people puzzled about why they feel so awful about themselves and why they are afraid to trust. It's as if we are born a blank slate, and no one ever writes on it letting us know who we are.

Healing involves recognizing the extent of the wounds, facing the pain, and taking the risk to engage in life-giving relationships. These steps will begin to satisfy long-neglected absences.

Type B trauma come from bad things happening.

- **The brain is seriously affected by "B" traumas in the memory area, so it seems right to call Type B traumas fractures of the mind**. If the bad events have left unresolved feelings or thoughts, the person cannot get back to a state of joy. That creates a fracture – a separation. Particularly bad events are mercifully forgotten, and amnesia protects the person from remembering them. Amnesia is an automatic brain function of instantly forgetting, that can be used protectively after age three. Before that, the brain is unable to establish a time or story line, so memories take a different form.

---

[2] Wilder, E. J., Friesen, J., Bierling, A.M., Koepcke, R., Poole, M. *Living From The Heart Jesus Gave You* (2013). Shepherd's House Inc. Used with permission.

- **When trauma reaches high intensity, it becomes overwhelming**. Before the person is conscious of what is happening, the trauma is forgotten, and a blank spot in one's memory appears. The person has no idea that the traumatic experience even happened. The person does not choose to forget the overwhelming episode, it is automatically lost to the memory. Although amnesia wipes away the pain for a time, it can be recovered at a later time. For healing to happen, the bad events need to be recovered and healed, so the blank spaces can be filled in.
- **If these memories are not recovered and healed, they begin to fester**. It takes finding the wound, opening the hurt feeling enough to understand the effect of the trauma, and praying that the Lord will bring full healing to the recovered memory.

Examples of Type A and Type B Traumas:

Type A Traumas:
1. Not being cherished or celebrated.
2. Not being delighted in.
3. Not having parents who draw out and speak positive things into your identity.
4. A lack of appropriate affection.
5. A lack of boundaries and limits.
6. Inadequate food, clothing, shelter, medical and dental care.
7. Not being taught how to do the hard things, sticking with something until you master it.
8. Lack of opportunity to develop personal resources and talents.

Type B Traumas:
2. Physical abuse.
3. Violent spanking, leaving bruises or emotional scars.
4. Sexual abuse, including inappropriate touching, voyeurism, pornography or an adult sharing sexual information.
5. Verbal abuse or name-calling.
6. Abandonment by a parent.
7. Torture or satanic ritual abuse.
8. Witnessing someone else being abused.

Psychological Trauma
- Psychological trauma is a type of damage to the mind and soul that occurs as a result of a severely distressing event.
- **Trauma is often the result of an overwhelming amount of stress that <u>exceeds one's ability to cope</u>, or integrate the emotions involved with that experience**.
- Includes an overwhelming experience (or repeated experiences), that is unexpectedly relived physiologically weeks, years and even decades later, as the person struggles to cope with their immediate circumstances. Such trauma almost always leads to serious, long-term negative consequences.

When Trauma Happens
- Disconnect occurs within the brain.
- Right brain shuts down and we are unable to access what the left brain knows.
- Our pain processing pathway gets stuck.
- Negative messages and negative experiences release harmful chemicals into our bodies that cause physical issues.

Role of the Vagus Nerve in Trauma

The word "vagus" means wandering in Latin - an appropriate name, as the vagus nerve is the longest cranial nerve. It runs all the way from the brain stem to the heart, stomach, kidneys, adrenals, intestines, and back to the brain again.

- "What happens in the vagus nerve doesn't stay in the vagus nerve."
- The vagus nerve sends out signals from your brainstem to your visceral organs.
- The vagus nerve is the captain of your inner parasympathetic nervous system. A healthy vagus nerve (without unprocessed trauma):
    - Prevents inflammation.
    - Helps make memories.
    - Helps you breathe.
    - Is involved with your heart.
    - Initiates the relaxation response.
    - Tells your brain how to feel.
- However, if we have unhealed trauma, we begin to experience all the physical symptoms of a former trauma when something triggers us. This is a big deal and very stressful every time it happens.
- The good news is that Jesus has made a way for us to heal from both Type A and Type B trauma. As we heal, those triggers decrease.

The Joy Center / Control Center

The right hemisphere contains the brain's control center (sometimes referred to as the joy center). The control center not only regulates motivation, it regulates emotion in a way that keeps us "ourselves," and that helps us stay present in the identity God has given us. The main emotions the control center regulates are joy and the big six unpleasant emotions: fear, anger, sadness, disgust, shame, and hopelessness.

The control center grows for as long as we live. What an amazing fact! Our creator God knew that many of us would experience trauma and, as a result, lack the good things He intends for us. So regardless of trauma, neglect, or lack of connection in our lives, He has provided a way within us to heal from trauma and receive the good we have been missing. What a loving God!

Physical vs. Emotional Pain

- Scientists have discovered that emotional pain can produce the same effects in the brain as physical pain.
- Trauma and dissociation happen with both Trauma A and Trauma B.
- Physical pain eventually subsides whereas emotional pain needs safe people and Jesus to heal.
- However, when someone is abandoned, shamed, rejected, or emotionally abused, it can be more difficult to heal from the emotional and psychological pain.

There are four levels in the control center:

- **The bottom level is the deep limbic structures:**
    - This part of our brain is always "on" and regulates the dopamine necessary for joy.
    - Here is the foundation of all attachments, and the basis for all relationships.
    - This part of the brain determines how well we function in life.
    - This part of the brain "lights up" when we feel the need to attach to someone.
    - If we do not receive a response in return, we feel rejected, unloved, abandoned, alone, and unwanted.
    - When unhealed, this part of the brain contributes greatly to addictions and poor sexual choices.
- **The next level is the amygdala:**
    - This is where our adrenaline is regulated. It is also connected to our immune system.
    - This level labels our world as good, bad, or scary, and where we decide to engage, fight, flee, or freeze.
    - When this part of our brain has been traumatized, it is not possible for us to engage appropriately, and we end up fighting, fleeing, or freezing.

- **The third level is the cingulate cortex:**
    - This level influences our interactions with others and synchronizes our internal life with the life around us.
    - The cingulate helps us adapt to others.
    - A healthy cingulate labels thing correctly and helps us respond appropriately.
    - This is where we have and build joy, where we return to peace from unpleasant emotions, and have mindsight with others (the ability to read others correctly and respond appropriately).
    - This is also where we regulate the big six unpleasant emotions: fear, anger, sadness, disgust, shame, and hopelessness.

- **And last, the top level is the right pre-frontal cortex:**
    - This is where identity, or "who I am," resides.
    - When the brain is properly developed, this part of the control center has executive control over the rest of the brain.
    - When healed and functioning properly, this part of the brain quiets us under stress, directs our moral choices, helps us be creative, helps us think with flexibility, and even influences our immune system.
    - It also helps us set and reach goals, and it holds our values and morals.

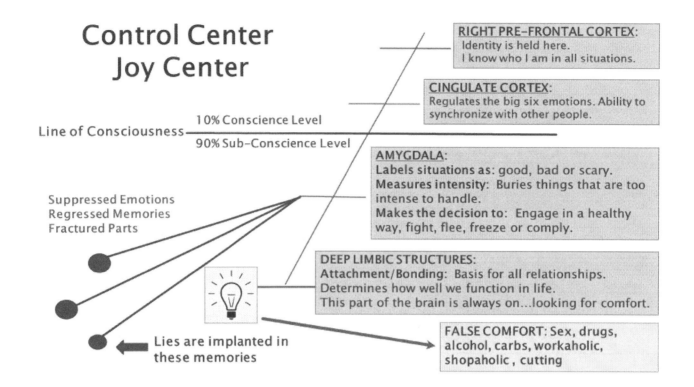

When the control center's capacity is limited:
- The control center acts like a fuse – if the current gets too strong, the weakest link gets fried, and the brain gets stuck.
- The control center acts like an amplifier – if emotions get too big, reality is distorted.
- The control center acts like a bridge – it carries relationship loads between people but collapses when relationships get too conflicted.
- The control center acts like a bucket – if you try to put too many emotions into the bucket, it will spill out everywhere.
- The control center acts like a mirror – it reflects how others see us and, when limited, makes us believe others see us as less than fully human.

Capacity is increased by practicing joy with others, but also by learning to be quiet with others. When you watch a healthy mother with her infant, the baby will look at the mother, smile, and coo, and when the baby has had enough it will look away. Babies who are ignored when they need attention and/or who are smothered with attention when they need quiet, can sometimes develop attachment disorders. **However, if a person has not received a healthy attachment, <u>it is still possible for them to receive it from others, even later in life.</u>**

<u>Remember</u>: this part of the brain continues to grow as we age. A brain with limited capacity will continue to pattern after a mature brain with healthy capacity.

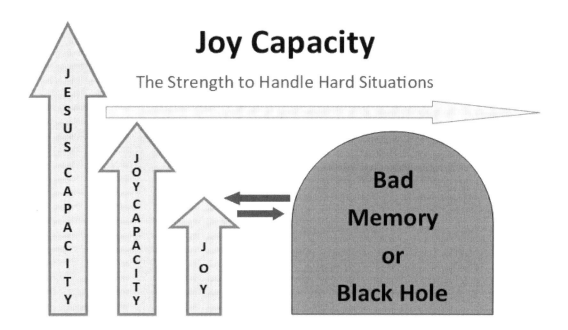

As we move towards wholeness and healing, we need to build our joy capacity. If we try to address a bad memory or fill the "black hole" from trauma, our brain will automatically "kick you out" of that area until you have enough joy capacity to handle that memory and trauma without being retraumatized.

HOW TO INCREASE YOUR JOY CAPACITY
- By practicing joy with other people.
- By learning to be quiet with others.
- Surround yourself with healthy, loving relationships.
- Learning to play and increase joy with people we love and trust.
- Grow in intimacy with the Lord.

This part of the brain continues to grow throughout life.

Relational Circuits

(The next sections *Relational Circuits*, *Joy and Well Being*, *The Joy Ring* and the *Joy* diagram are adaptations of the teachings of Margaret Webb and Dr Karl Lehman, as cited in *Immanuel Lifestyle Group Workbook*[3])

Our brains have circuits that guide our relational connections with God and with others.

These circuits are formed and are changed through relationships.

What is it like to have our relational circuits off?

- I just want to make a problem, person, or feeling go away.
- I don't want to listen to what others feel or say.
- My mind is locked onto something upsetting.
- I don't want to be connected to the person I usually like.
- I just want to get away, fight, or freeze.
- I aggressively interrogate, judge, and try to fix others.

What is it like to have our relational circuits on?

- The person is more important than the problem.
- I can be respectful, aware of, and interested in another's point of view.
- I see this moment as a new situation where I can learn something.
- I am not struggling with feeling isolated and alone.
- I can join in give-and-take, both verbally and nonverbally.
- I am eager to talk with God about this situation – stay connected with Immanuel.

Exercises to turn on our relational circuits.

- The Moro Reflex (startled, angry, or scared - repeat 4 times).
- First Aid Yawn (alternate facing right and left - repeat 4 times).
- Attachment Center Exercise (breathe in and tap, breathe out and massage - repeat 4 times).

When I am afraid, I will trust in you, oh Lord. - Psalm 56:3

Gratitude also turns on our relational circuits

Discuss: Can you think of a time this past week when your relational circuits were "shut down" or "shut off"?

How does that compare to times when your circuits were "on"?

---

[3] *Immanuel Lifestyle Small Group Workbook* (2015), p 25, 63-64. Alive and Well, Inc. Used with permission.

Joy and Well Being

The Bible tells us, *The joy of the Lord is your strength.* - Nehemiah 8:10

The definition of Joy is relational connection. *"Someone is glad to be with me."*

Joy is a relational experience that is the basis for spiritual experience, human bonding, healthy growth in identity and good health generally. Joy is the feeling many people experience as "falling in love" with their baby, their grandchild, their first love, a puppy, and a face that just lights up to see you.

No one seeks treatment for joy reduction. No one worries about loved ones who are just too joyful. The problem is that people who are failing to thrive have issues, they live in conflict, and do not seem to know or remember that joy would be a natural and rewarding way to live.

One of the first goals in creating a family, a community or a recovery group is to build the group around joy. While many groups form around a shared fear or problem, this is not a desirable long-term plan. Joy is our deepest motivation and need. Joy needs to be the way we live. When trauma and abuse survivors change their main goal from dealing with trauma to building joyful lives, it often leads to a remarkable reduction in crises and the need for hospitalization.

The Joy Ring

Look at the diagram on the next page. The 6 emotions on the "islands" around "JOY" are hardwired into the brain from birth. God created them for a positive purpose and to help us as we experience challenging or dangerous circumstances.

- Anger – fight a threat to safety.
- Fear – flee from danger.
- Sad – alert to the loss of something/someone important (a need).
- Disgust – avoidance of something harmful.
- Shame – alert to mis-attunement (feeling out of sync with another person).
- Hopeless despair – stop trying something that can't work.
- Joy – seeing that another person is glad to see me or be with me.

Joy is in the center, but it is not hardwired at birth. **Joy must be developed in relationship, which is evidence that we are made in the image of God**. The neuronal pathways back to relational joy are formed in relationship.

To the extent that we get stuck on any of the 6 islands without a bridge back to relational connection and joy, we lack the capacity to respond well to challenging relationships and circumstances.

Fortunately, capacity can be built or rebuilt through relational encounters with Jesus and others.

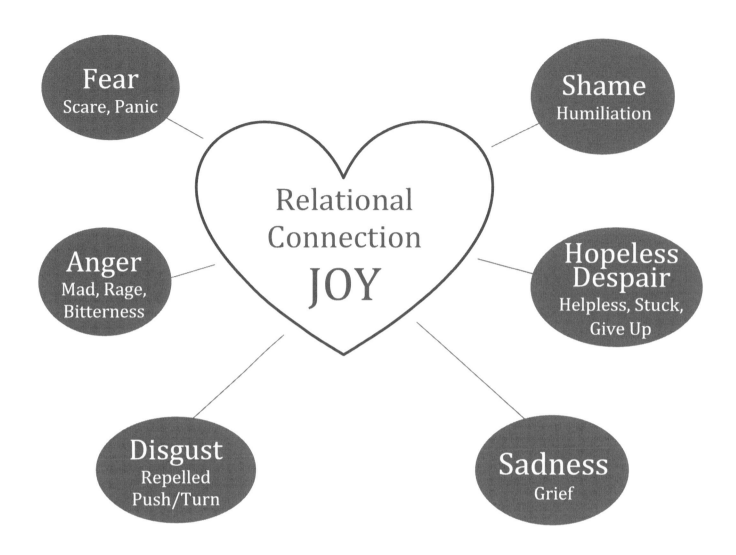

Building a bridge back to joy and being able to return to joy from a painful emotion, does not mean that we're "over the top" happy. It means that during the challenges in life, we know that someone (Jesus) is glad to be with us!

Step Two
Homework & Journaling

Step Two: I will begin to recognize that God's plan and design for me is to grow in JOY and to be relationally connected to Him and to others.

1. What does wholeness mean to me? What would it look and feel like?

2. Do I believe God has the power to make me whole? Why or why not?

3. When I think about my relational circuits, are they mostly on or off in my relationship with God? Do I experience joy in my relationship with God?

4. When I think about my relational circuits, are they mostly on or off in my relationships with people who are close to me?

5. When do I experience joy the most?

6. Think of a time this week when you noticed your relational circuits were "off." Briefly describe what happened in that situation.

7. Think of a time this week when you noticed your relational circuits were "on." Briefly describe what happened in that situation and how it was different from the situation described in question #6.

8. Write a prayer to God asking for His help.

Appreciation/Gratitude Exercises

You might want to start a journal and answer these questions on a regular basis in your journal.

1. What do I appreciate about God?
2. What do I appreciate about myself (how God created me)?
3. What am I grateful for today?
4. Who am I grateful for today?

Step Three: God's Plan for Me

Step Three: I will begin to explore the purpose of God's plan for a better life. This life does not include physical, emotional, mental, spiritual, or sexual abuse.

Jeremiah 29:11 *For I know the plans I have for you, declares the Lord, plans to prosper you and not to harm you, plans to give you a hope and a future.*

Isaiah 32:18 *My people will live in peaceful places, in secure homes, in undisturbed places of rest.*

God waits for you to seek His ways and to participate in His plan for you. After salvation, you're to seek Him and to partner with Him to receive the abundant life and wholeness He has promised you.

> *During all the years I lived in abuse, I trusted the Lord and believed He would rescue me, and my husband would change. It seems ludicrous now, but I somehow thought the Lord would swoop down and miraculously take me out of the situation. It wasn't until many years later that I realized God was asking me to do my part. I needed to be an active participant in His plan for my life.*
> --Diane Stores, Door of Hope Founder

In so many ways, you have cut yourself off from the world and created another world to live in. Rather than living in the joyful world God has invited you into, you have created a confining world; a world with little pleasure or fulfillment. Joy escapes you and you feel alone, forgotten, and defective.

Abuse: A Slow Boil

Abuse doesn't usually happen suddenly. It's like the illustration of the frog and the pot of water. When you put a frog into a pot of boiling water, it will immediately jump out. However, if you put a frog in a pot of cool water and slowly turn up the temperature, it will stay still and boil to death. Abuse has been like this for so many of us. It starts slowly and eventually permeates your soul. One day, you wake up and realize you're dying and you're not sure how you got here. The abuse you've been experiencing may have been going on for many years, maybe even since you were a child. If so, you've been conditioned to being treated this way and may not even know there's a different way, a better way, God's way.

When you learn as a young child that you can't speak up, and that you can't talk about the "bad" things, you eventually bury that pain deep inside of you and retreat behind your walls of protection. You shut down. You never learn what it means to make healthy choices. You never learn how to process your emotions in constructive ways. Eventually, you don't even know what you want or need.

When you don't know what you want or need, and when you don't know God's plan for your life, you will follow the plan others set for you.

Power and Control Wheel

At the end of this chapter (p.40), you'll find the Power and Control Wheel, created by the *Domestic Abuse Intervention Project in Duluth, Minnesota*. It was developed through work with women attending local support and educational groups and is based on their lived experiences with abuse. Over time, they were able to name the tactics that were being used against them on a daily basis, and thus created the Power and Control Wheel image. This wheel gives a powerful picture of how abuse and control can operate. It outlines the various types of abuse and control and gives examples of how each function.

God's plan for relationships looks very different. His plan is one based on mutual respect. The following chart shows comparisons between a life of abuse and survival, and a life lived by God's plan. God's Word tells us that He wants you to live in freedom and safety. He wants to come into your deepest places and replace the lies you've believed with His Truth. He wants to wash away all your pain and sorrow. He calls you precious, beloved, and chosen.

Living with Abuse Versus Living in God's Freedom

A Relationship Based on Power & Control	God's Plan for Relationship
Minimizes, Denies, Blames	Listens, Respects, Supports
Leads to Dishonesty, Hiding, and Distrust	Leads to Honesty, Openness, and Trust
Uses Words to Bring the Other Down	Uses Words to Build the Other Up
Male Privilege	Mutual and Shared Responsibility
Uses Coercion and Threats	Uses Negotiation and Fairness
Uses Intimidation	Displays Safe and Non-Threatening Behavior
The Weak are Taken Advantage Of	The Weak Become Strong in God
Isolates	Builds True and Lasting Community
Your World Goes from Light to Dark	Your World Goes from Dark to Light
You Move from Liberty to Bondage	You Move from Bondage to Liberty
Brings You from Life to Death	Brings You from Death to Life
Based on Fear	Based on Love

Understanding Abuse

Submit to one another out of reverence to Christ.
Malachi 2:16 Ephesians 5:21 Ephesians 5:21-23

Abuse is a pattern of behavior in a relationship that is used to gain and/or maintain power and control over another person.

Domestic Abuse is About Control, Not Anger

Many people think that domestic abuse is about one person in a relationship getting angry and hitting, punching, and beating his or her partner. That's the face of abuse often seen. But domestic abuse is much more than that.

For starters, it's not about anger. Everyone gets angry, but not everyone is abusive.

The real issue underlying domestic abuse is the perpetrator's need to feel powerful and in control of another person's behaviors and actions. Perpetrators believe that they are entitled to be in charge of the relationship, and that it is okay for them to use any means – even physical and psychological intimidation – to remain in control.

In short, domestic abuse isn't an anger management issue; it's an intentional choice to use violence to feel powerful and to control another person to get what they want.

Domestic abuse isn't always physical. In fact, some victims don't recognize the abuse because they don't have bruises. However, name calling, insults, put-downs, social and economic isolation, threats, and other techniques can be as effective as fists. Abused women often remark that bruises heal, but words erode the heart and the soul.

Controlling behavior can take many forms, from subtle to extreme. Your partner may simply announce, "I have the remote and I'm in charge of the TV." Or they may start forbidding you to go out, have your own money, or socialize with friends without permission. In more extreme forms, they may threaten to do something dire, such as take away your children or intimidate you by displaying weapons or smashing things in the house. Some abusers create fear and intimidation by requiring their partner to justify the mileage on the car's odometer; checking caller ID to see who has called; requiring approval on outfits before you wear them; and calling at certain times to prove that you're where you said you would be.

Those who abuse insist on making all the decisions within the relationship without consulting their partners, or in opposition to their partner's wishes or opinions. These decisions can include such things as choosing how to spend family income or where to go on vacation.

According to experts in the field, domestic abuse is seriously under-reported and undiagnosed.

Cycle of Violence/Abuse

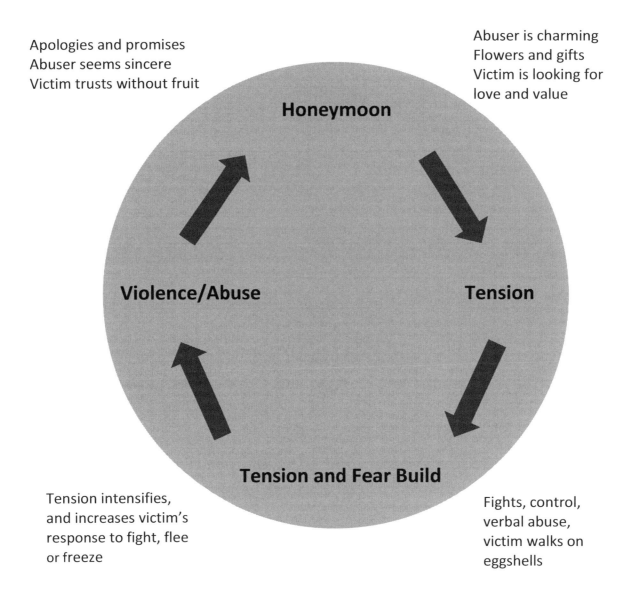

Apologies and promises
Abuser seems sincere
Victim trusts without fruit

Abuser is charming
Flowers and gifts
Victim is looking for love and value

Tension intensifies, and increases victim's response to fight, flee or freeze

Fights, control, verbal abuse, victim walks on eggshells

Note: This cycle gets shorter and shorter until the honeymoon part disappears

Types of Abuse

Emotional Abuse

Emotional abuse includes hurting another's feelings by name-calling and making cruel and unfair comments. It can be very intimidating and can affect our God-given identity.

Examples include:

- Cursing, swearing, and/or screaming at you.
- Repeated harassment, interrogation, or degradation.
- Attacks on self-esteem, and/or insults to your person (name-calling, put-downs, ridicule).
- Attacks and/or insults about people you care for, your family, or friends.
- Threatening to "get" you or your family.
- Controlling and/or limiting your behavior (i.e. keeping you from using the phone, or seeing friends; not letting you leave the room or house; following you; monitoring or limiting your phone conversations; checking the mileage on your car; keeping you from material, ideas, activities, and places that they do not like).
- Interrupting you while you are eating or preventing you from eating.
- Forcing you to stay awake, or to get up from sleep.
- Blaming you for everything that goes wrong.
- Forcing you to do degrading things (i.e. making you kneel, making you beg for money).
- Using the difference in physical size to intimidate you.
- Criticizing your thoughts, feelings, opinions, beliefs, and actions.
- Treating you like a servant or "underling" regarding household chores and decisions.
- Being extremely jealous, constantly accusing you of flirting or cheating.
- Spitting at or near you.
- Controlling how extra money is spent; forcing you to ask for and account for money you get; or acting like the work you do at home is of no economic value to the family.
- Telling you that you are "sick" and need therapy.
- Using physical disabilities against you or putting you down for your disability.

Psychological Abuse

Psychological abuse is any threat to do bodily harm to a partner, a child, a family member, friend, pet, or one's self (suicide). It elicits hurt, anger, fear, and degradation and makes you question your self-worth. It also renders you helpless and/or unable to escape further physical, sexual, or psychological abuse.

Examples include:
- Threatening to punch, hit, slap, or kick.
- Threatening to use a weapon.
- Threatening to harm himself/herself if you leave.
- Threatening to punish your children to "get back" at you.
- Threatening to harm your children and/or harm a pet to "get back" at you.
- Throwing objects in your direction.
- Vague threats, such as "You're going to get it," or "I'm really going to let you have it."
- Smashing and breaking things.
- Throwing objects around the room.
- Punching walls, slamming doors.
- Hiding, stealing, or destroying your possessions.
- Sabotaging your car.
- Any emotional abuse which, in the past, was a prelude to physical or sexual abuse.

Physical Abuse

Physical Abuse is any non-accidental use of force that results in bodily injury, pain, or impairment. This includes, but is not limited to, being slapped, burned, cut, bruised, or improperly physically restrained. Physical abuse happens to children and adults of all ages. Neglect is also physical abuse and can be present when one adult is responsible for caring for another (i.e. adult child caring for a parent).

Examples include:
- Restraining or restricting movement.
- Slapping or punching.
- Kicking or pushing.
- Burning, cutting, or stabbing.
- Choking or biting.
- Shooting with a weapon.
- Withholding food or medical treatment.
- Forcing a person to take drugs or drugging them without their knowledge.
- Denying sleep.
- Inflicting pain on other people or animals.

Sexual Abuse

Any non-consenting sexual act or behavior.

Examples include:
- You indicate "no" and your limits are not respected.
- You are sleeping.
- You are drunk or high and are unable to say "no."
- You are afraid to say "no."
- Insisting that you dress in a more sexual or modest way than you want to dress.
- Making demands about how you dress.
- Making demeaning remarks about your body and/or body parts.
- Minimizing your feelings about sex.
- Berating you about your sexual history.

Gaslighting Abuse

Gaslighting is a form of abuse that causes frequent doubt regarding one's thoughts, experiences, perceptions, and decisions. This abuse is generally gradual, and sometimes subtle in nature, leading one to constantly feel beat down and exhausted, but not able to explain why or put a name to it.

Examples include:
- Behaviors that cause you to believe your needs and thoughts are not valid, such as negative body language, negative looks, or ignoring you.
- Withholding emotions to gain control over you and causing you to believe your emotions are irrational or invalid.
- Denying past conversations or events as if they never happened or did not happen the way you remember.
- Treating you like a child.
- Degrading comments that attack your character and lead you to feel that you are stupid, or inadequate.
- Manipulating situations to purposefully cause you self-doubt and confusion (i.e. telling you their favorite color is blue then, with other people, changing it to yellow, in the attempt to try to make you look like a fool or incompetent).
- Every decision made is criticized and put into a negative context, often leading you to believe you can't make good decisions. After a while, you begin to shut down, feel frozen, and may withdraw from activities, friends, and society, as you become increasingly confused and exhausted.
- Constantly being told you are crazy, your thoughts are crazy, you can't remember anything right, your thoughts are wrong, the way you choose to do things is wrong.

- Many times, they use subtle, manipulative words that aren't forthright, but contain seeds of doubt and negativity. They may use other subtle ways, like a look or certain body language.
- Regularly being corrected or told/shown that there are better ways to perform tasks or make decisions, as though your way is inadequate or insufficient.
- Controlling conversations.
- Reverting questions back to you to take attention off them, further causing you to question your motives and views.
- Accuse you of trying to do what they are doing to you or projecting back onto you (i.e. accusing you of cheating, trying to confuse you, etc.).

Additional signs include:
- Constantly second guessing yourself, even in simple decisions like what to cook for dinner; wondering if you can do anything right.
- Feeling confused or crazy in situations outside the relationship. It starts to permeate every area of your life.
- Depression sets in and you begin to lose hope and joy, often sensing you used to be fun and confident. You are not sure why you're depressed, because nothing is really that bad. You can't put a finger on it.
- You begin to question your value and worth.

Spiritual Abuse

In their book, *The Subtle Power of Spiritual Abuse*[4], David Johnson and Jeff Van Vonderen, define spiritual abuse as mistreating one in need of help, support, or spiritual empowerment, resulting in the weakening, undermining, or decreasing of one's spiritual strength.

Spiritual abuse...

- Happens when one in authority uses their spiritual position to control or dominate you.
- Involves overriding your feelings and opinions, without regard for what will result in your life, emotions, or spiritual well-being.
- Uses spirituality/religion to make you live up to a "spiritual standard."
- Promotes external performance, without regard for your well-being, or is used as a means of proving your spiritual maturity.
- Uses Scripture as a weapon, to keep you submissive.

---

[4] Johnson, D. & Van Vonderen, J. (2005) *The Subtle Power of Spiritual Abuse*. Bloomington, MN: Bethany House Publishers.

Anatomy of Spiritual Abuse
- Power dynamic: assumes that the helper is healthier and more knowledgeable.
- Focus subtly changes from the issue to the person (your position before God is questioned, and you feel judged).
- Your questions to authority bring feelings of being judged. Manipulation surfaces when you ask an honest question and the one in authority pulls rank on you. Example: "I'm the authority and because I'm the authority, I'm not to be questioned." This attitude is a big red flag. (Questioning does not make you wrong. Authority doesn't mean one's thoughts and opinions are superior.)

Characteristics of a Spiritually Abusive System
- **Power positioning**: Distorted image of God; high levels of anxiety; people pleasing; high need to be punished or pay for mistakes; ignore your insights because you're made to feel "too critical"; high need for structure; difficulty saying "no"; allowing others to take advantage of you.
- **Performance:** can't make or admit mistakes; have a view of God that says it's more important how you act than who you are; can't rest; sense of self-righteousness or shame; negative view of self; difficulty forgiving self; difficulty receiving grace.
- **Unspoken rules**: saying things in code instead of saying them plainly; talking about people instead of to them; reading other meanings into what people say.
- **Lack of balance**: high need to control others; out of touch with feelings; guess at what is normal; stress-related illness; let unsafe people come close; extreme forms of denial.
- **Paranoia**: sense that something is wrong, or that someone is upset and you've caused it; if there's a problem, believing you have to solve it; feeling like no one understands you; afraid to take healthy risks; suspicious and afraid of others; putting up boundaries that keep safe people away; feelings of guilt when you haven't done anything wrong; difficulty trusting people.
- **Misplaced loyalty**: high need to be right; critical of others; giving others the "third degree"; narrow minded; fear of being abandoned; possessive in relationships.
- **Code of silence**: self-analytical; rebelling against structure; feeling alone; living a double life; message carrier for people; can't ask for help.

Effects of Spiritual Abuse
- Feelings of guilt and shame.
- Easily controlled through fear and manipulation.
- Damage to spiritual integrity.
- Diminished ability to relate to others and isolation.
- Dependent upon the will of the abuser.
- Loss of confidence in yourself and your standing with God apart from the abuser.
- Emotionally enslaved to the abusive one.
- Lack of healthy personal boundaries.

Power and Control Wheel

Step Three
Homework & Journaling

Step Three: I will begin to explore the purpose of God's plan for a better life. This life does not include physical, emotional, mental, spiritual, or sexual abuse.

1. What behaviors or beliefs did I experience in my family of origin (positive or negative)? How did these experiences affect how I see myself?

2. Do I see similarities in the way I was treated as a child and what I have experienced as an adult? If so, how?

3. How has abuse in my life been destructive to me? To others?

4. How has abuse affected how I can/cannot experience freedom in my everyday situations?

5. How has abuse affected how I respond to and/or treat other people?

6. If I could design an "ideal" plan for my life, what would it look like?

7. Write myself a letter about what I think God would say to me about His plan.

Step Four: I am God's Child and I am Being Renewed in His Image

Step Four: I am willing to see myself as a spiritual being, a special child of God who can learn to love, respect, and care for myself.

I recognize the need to identify negative attitudes, defense mechanisms, and feelings connected to my abuse.

Genesis 1:27 *So God created man in His own image; in the image of God He created him; male and female, He created them.*

Ephesians 1: 5 *He predestined us to be adopted as His sons through Jesus Christ in accordance with His pleasure and His will.*

Psalm 139:23-24 *Search me, O God, and know my heart; test me and know my anxious thoughts. See if there is any offensive way in me, and lead me in the way everlasting.*

Lamentations 3:40 *Let us examine our ways and test them, and let us return to the Lord.*

Learning to Love and Care for Yourself

God is willing, and able, to change you from the inside out and give you His perspective, but you need to learn how to love, respect, and care for yourself as well.

All people struggle at times with feelings of inadequacy and low self-worth. But those who have lived with abuse have a greater challenge. Mark 12:31 tells us to love our neighbor as ourselves.

It seems important to God in this verse that we extend the same love and grace to ourselves as we do to others.

Discuss: Why is it that we can have grace for others but deny ourselves the same thing?

What are some things you can do in the area of selfcare that have been neglected in the past?

Loving Yourself vs Selfishness

One of the great paradoxes in life, as well as in relationships, is the concept of loving yourself and the concept of selfishness. Oftentimes, there's confusion in reconciling these two.

There is no real relationship with another without loving yourself first. Without self-love, you are not able to give love to another. Nor are you able to receive love from others. The depth of your ability to love yourself will determine how deeply you can enter relationship, and really love another.

To truly love yourself, you must know how God sees you. Humility is agreeing with God about who He says you are – no more, no less. And He believes you are worth dying for. The more you walk in the Truth of God's love, and let that permeate you and pour through you, the more you can love yourself and then love others. Apart from God you can do nothing (John 15:5) but with Him, and His amazing love pouring through you, you can live the life He wants you to have. A life of freedom, secure in His love.

"Love yourself" is not referring to the prideful, worldly type of loving oneself (also known as self-worship); **but is about being thankful and appreciating the person God made you to be**. The two could not be more different! True humility is accepting what God says about you, accepting who He says you are.

Discuss: What do you appreciate about yourself?

The level of bondage that results from self-rejection, self-hatred, and/or unwillingness to forgive yourself is shocking. Below are just a few of the symptoms:

- Self-rejection: not accepting yourself, always beating up on yourself, not happy with the person God made you to be, etc.
- Self-hatred: hating the person God made you to be, considering yourself ugly, dumb, clumsy, etc.
- Unforgiveness or bitterness: continuing to hold things against yourself, such as something in your past that was embarrassing, gross, or that you are still ashamed of (even after repentance).
- Being hard on yourself mentally, physically, or emotionally. Always seeing yourself as worthless or pushing to reach irrational goals just to feel good about yourself.
- Low self-esteem: always seeing yourself as a failure, or less than those around you.
- Seeing yourself as ugly, worthless, stupid, etc.

Questions to consider:

- Did God create your physical body? If so, would you say that God made an ugly body?
- Did God create your mind and intellect? If so, would you say God created a dumb, stupid, or worthless brain?
- If God created you in His image, would you say that His image is dumb, stupid, worthless, or ugly?

David was a humble man with a heart after God's own heart, yet he praised and thanked God for the marvelous work that God had made (referring to his physical body): *"I will praise thee; for I am fearfully and wonderfully made: marvelous are thy works; and that my soul knows right well."* Psalms 139:14

David is not boasting about himself, but is being thankful, and is rejoicing over the beautiful creation that God made in him! How many who consider themselves ugly are looking at things the way David did? Probably not too many!

Instead of saying, "I'm ugly," David said, "Wow! Look at what God gave me! It's marvelous!"

It's vital that you let God transform your mind, so that you can have the same attitude about what God's given you. Be patient, though, as this is a process and will take time.

Thought Life

As you go through the healing process it is very important that you become aware of what's going on in your thinking. Are your thoughts lining up to God's thoughts? Are you thinking what He thinks about you?

The more aware you are of what's going on in your thoughts, the more aware you can be of taking thoughts captive when they don't line up to what God says about you.

2 Corinthians 10:4-6: *The weapons we fight with are not the weapons of the world. On the contrary, they have divine power to demolish strongholds. We demolish arguments and every pretension that sets itself up against the knowledge of God, and we take captive every thought to make it obedient to Christ. And we will be ready to punish every act of disobedience, once your obedience is complete.*

Action Step: Take your thoughts captive. Every time a thought floats through your mind that doesn't line up with God's Word, find a scripture verse that addresses it, write it on a note card, and speak it aloud.

You are made in God's image. He spoke the world into being. As you speak His Word you are creating a spiritual reality. You are agreeing with Him and telling the enemy that you will no longer partner with him against yourself. You're standing on God's Word!

After all, God created you and, as your Creator, He's the only one that gets to define you.

Romans 12:2 *Do not conform to the pattern of this world, but be transformed by the renewing of your mind. Then you will be able to test and approve what God's will is—his good, pleasing and perfect will.*

Defense Mechanisms

It is now time to identify the things that might be holding you back and keeping you from knowing and following God's ways. If you want to end the confusion and dysfunction in your life, you must recognize what has been negative, so you can replace it with something better like God's ways are higher and better than yours, and He is your only source of real Hope.

Defense mechanisms are clever ways you protect yourself. Some of them you may have knowingly constructed, while others may have been in place since you were a very small child. They have helped you hide in uncomfortable situations.

Let's look at some common defense mechanisms, as we go through them, try to identify which of these you relate with the most.

- **Denial** is a psychological defense mechanism that refuses to admit the truth or the reality that something is sad or painful.
- **Minimizing** accepts that there is a problem but refuses to acknowledge how severe it is or how devastating its effects.
- **Blaming** puts the responsibility for problems on other people or other situations. It prevents you from looking at your part in the problem and keeps you from seeking solutions.

- **Excusing** offers justifications and explanations for your behavior or the behavior of others.
- **Dodging** changes the conversation to avoid threatening or painful topics. Dodging deflects us from addressing the real issues.
- **Attacking** keeps others away when they begin to see into the reality of your life. Anger can be a powerful defense in keeping others out and isolation in place.
- **Projection** eases guilt. You take your own toxic emotions, like jealousy, and project them onto the other person.
- **Rationalizing** helps you not feel at odds with a situation. It's an attempt to prove to yourself that something really isn't that big, or that painful.
- **Fantasy** can help you create an internal world that is much more satisfying than the reality in which you live.
- **Isolation** keeps others out so they will not see what is really going on in your life. It also keeps you from having to accept that reality.
- **Rescuing** or becoming a caretaker for the needs of others and neglecting your own needs. Your focus might be on people-pleasing and performing.

Many of us use defense mechanisms because we still don't trust that God will protect us and care for us. While defense mechanisms do help keep people out, they also build walls between you and God. For you to move forward into all God has for you, these walls of self-protection must come down.

Defense mechanisms keep you from exploring your own life. They hinder you from recognizing your strengths, addressing areas of weakness, and discovering your unique personality – all of which contribute to a rich and full life. Please understand: God loves you perfectly – through and through – however, your ability to experience this love, and its ability to transform you is inhibited when you relate to God from behind walls and masks. God deals with truth, and you can experience that love more profoundly when you are authentic.

Lowering your walls can be very scary, but it is necessary if you want to grow in your relationships.

Ridding yourself of your defense mechanisms, and letting God protect you is a process. It doesn't happen overnight, but God will be faithful to you in this process. He, more than anyone, wants to see you live in the full potential He planned for you. You will learn that you no longer need to hide from God or others – no longer have to cover your nakedness, your shame. You will experience God's love and acceptance when you are at your best, but also at your worst.

In embracing your broken parts, with God's help, you will be transformed, healed, and set free to live genuinely. It also frees you to love others (and God) in a deeper, more genuine way.

What God Says

You Say	God Says	Scripture
It's impossible.	All things are possible.	Luke 18:27
I'm too tired.	I will give you rest.	Matthew 11:28-30
Nobody loves me.	I love you.	John 3:16 & John 3:34
I can't go on.	My grace is sufficient.	2 Corinthians 12:9
I can't figure things out.	I will direct your steps.	Proverbs 3:5-6
I can't do it.	You can do all things.	Philippians 4:13
I'm not able.	I am able.	2 Corinthians 9:8
It's not worth it.	It will be worth it.	Romans 8:28
I can't forgive myself.	I forgive you.	1 John 1:9
I can't manage.	I will supply all your needs.	Philippians 4:19
I'm afraid.	I have not given you a spirit of fear.	2 Timothy 1:7
I'm always worried and frustrated.	Cast all your cares upon me.	I Peter 5:7
I'm not smart enough.	I give you wisdom.	1 Corinthians 1:30
I feel all alone.	I will never leave you or forsake you.	Hebrews 13:5

Remember Who You Are

Our loving Father has given you hundreds of scriptures naming who you are in Christ. Over and over He says, "Remember who you are!"

Take time each day to gaze into His face, meditate on these scriptures and let Him show you how He sees you.

You are Abba's child
Galatians 4:6 *Because you are sons, God sent the Spirit of His Son into our hearts, the Spirit who calls out, "Abba Father."*

Romans 8:15 *You received the Spirit of sonship. And by Him we cry, "Abba, Father."*

You are on the winning side
Colossians 2:15 *Having disarmed the powers and authorities, He made a public spectacle of them, triumphing over them by the cross.*

He is the victorious warrior
Exodus 15:3 *The Lord is the warrior; the Lord is His name.*

You are crowned with love and compassion
Psalm 103:4 *...who redeems your life from the pit and crowns you with love and compassion.*

You are rich in His grace
2 Corinthians 8:9 *You know the grace of our Lord Jesus Christ, that though He was rich, yet for our sakes He became poor.*

You are free from condemnation
Romans 8:1 *There is now no condemnation for those who are in Christ Jesus.*

You are heard
Isaiah 65:24 *Before they call I will answer; while they are still speaking I will hear.*

He delights in you
Zephaniah 3:17 *The Lord your God is with you, He is mighty to save. He will take great delight in you, He will quiet you with His love, He will rejoice over you with singing.*

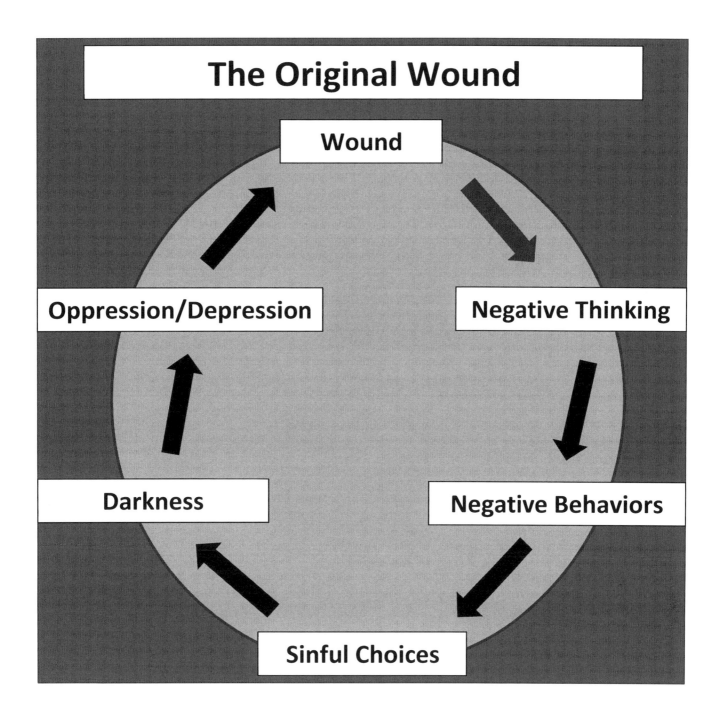

Many times, we try to "fix" behaviors and symptoms that are caused initially by trauma or a significant wound in our heart. When we focus on healing the root issue of the wound, then our thinking processes, behaviors, choices, and resulting oppression/depression will also start to heal and change.

How Our Roots Can Affect Our Fruit

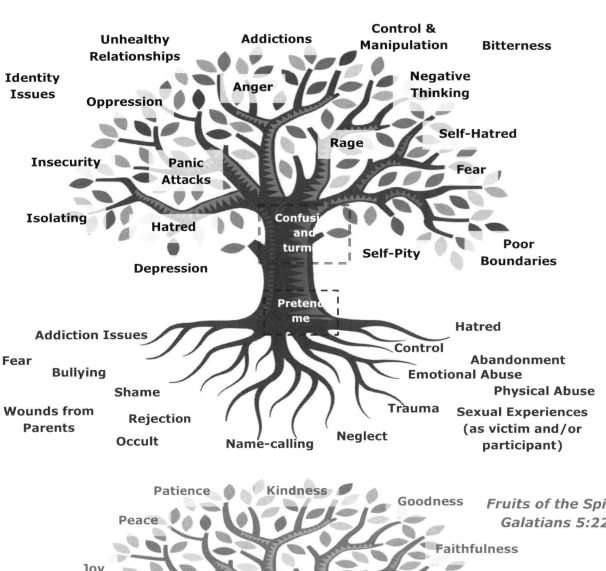

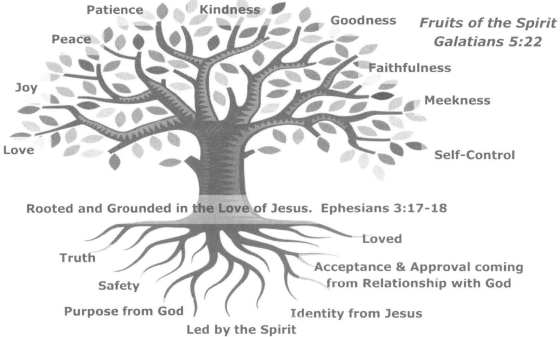

Step Four
Homework & Journaling

Step Four: I am willing to see myself as a spiritual being, a special child of God who can learn to love, respect, and care for myself.

I recognize the need to identify negative attitudes, defense mechanisms, and feelings connected to my abuse.

1. What was I like as a child? What did I like? Dislike? What did I want to be when I grew up?

2. What things from childhood have shaped who I am today?

3. Circle the following feelings and behaviors I've had from being abused:

    Shame, fear, rage, anger, bitterness, self-hatred, distrust, depression, manipulation of others, dishonesty, denial, chemical use, promiscuity, avoidance of men, isolation, bulimia, anorexia, overeating, suicidal thoughts or attempts, anxiety, abusive to others

    What other responses have I had?

4. Do I feel like I still might have a need for any of these behaviors for self-protection? Are there any I would like to change? If so, which ones?

5. How would I like God to see me? How would I like to see myself?

6. What can I do to nurture that special creation I am? (What activities will increase my Joy Capacity?)

7. What do I need to do to prioritize healthy selfcare options that will help me to take better care of myself and grow closer to Jesus?

Step Five: Identify What I Need to Take Responsibility For

Step 5: I will identify areas where I need to take responsibility.

The person who abused me is responsible for the abusive acts committed against me. I will not accept the guilt and shame resulting from those acts.

Psalm 34:4-5 *I sought the Lord and He answered me. He delivered me from all my fears. Those who look to Him are radiant; their faces are never covered with shame.*

John 8:32 *Then you will know the truth, and the truth will set you free.*

As you continue your recovery process it is important you begin to identify what is guilt and what is shame. Too often, in an abusive situation, the victim takes on the shame that should belong to the one who was abusive. God will help you separate the things that don't belong to you from those things you need to ask forgiveness for and turn from.

Guilt vs False Guilt

Guilt is felt when you realize you've sinned. False guilt occurs when sin has been repented of and forgiven, but Satan keeps it before you, to induce shame (seeing yourself as a failure). True guilt or conviction will prompt you to repent and turn from your sin. False guilt is used by Satan to rip apart the lives of countless believers around the world.

Robert Walter in, *If I've Been Forgiven, Why Do I Still Feel Bad?* writes:

The cross has two arms. With one arm of the cross, God reaches out to forgive our guilty behavior. With the other arm, God reaches out to embrace our shameful sense of being. He forgives and He heals. He gives us a new start AND a new identity. He hates our sin AND He loves us unconditionally. God gives us purpose and joy, abundance and peace, love and freedom. The gospel is forgiveness and it's a whole lot more: Healing, Restoring, Washing, Renewing, Regenerating, Delivering, Protecting, and Equipping.[5]

As you identify the areas you need to take responsibility for and repent of, it will become clearer which things don't belong to you. You can then release those things to the Lord. They were never yours in the first place.

Shame

Shame is the painful feeling arising from the consciousness of something dishonorable or improper, done by you or by someone else.

Shame is the raincoat of the soul, repelling the living water that would otherwise establish us as the beloved of God. It prevents us from receiving grace and truth where we need them most."[6]
- Robert Walter, from "If I've Been Forgiven Why Do I Still Feel Bad?"

It leaves you feeling dirty, worthless, and that you're a failure. As a result, you feel unworthy to approach God and have the intimate relationship He wants to have with you!

---

[5] Walter, R. *If I've Been Forgiven, Why Do I Still Feel Bad?* From ongodstrail.com/why-do-i-still-feel-bad Used with permission.
[6] Ibid. Used with permission.

While guilt is seeing what you've done, shame is seeing yourself as a failure. Guilt is looking at the sin, shame is attacking your **identity**. If you allow yourself to meditate on guilt, it will turn into shame. **If not properly dealt with, guilt turns into the stronghold called shame.**

When God convicts you of something you have done outside of His Will, He will always focus on the behavior. He also gives us a "way out." In **1 John 1:9** we read, *If we confess our sins, he is faithful and just and will forgive us our sins and purify us from all unrighteousness.*

When Satan brings false guilt about something in our past, he will always focus on our identity.

God's voice will sound like this, "My child, what you are involved in is not who you are. It is not my will for your life."

He will be there with open arms ready to receive you and love you into wholeness.

Satan's voice will sound like this, "There you go again. You really are defective. You might as well give up."

Satan's voice will tear you down, **God's voice will build you up.**

Separating the two voices can be very challenging in the beginning of your healing journey. You may have gotten so used to the condemning voice that it's hard to hear God's voice in the clamber and noisiness.

Although shame and guilt may seem similar, shame is highly correlated with addiction, depression, eating disorders, aggression, violence, bullying, and suicide. In contrast, guilt is linked to empathy, and understanding other perspectives.

Shame is a focus on self, guilt is a focus on behavior. Guilt is, "I did something bad." Shame is, "I am bad." Guilt: "I'm sorry. I made a mistake." Shame: "I'm sorry. I am a mistake."

Dealing with Shame – Dr. Brené Brown

Dr. Brené Brown, a leading researcher on shame, reveals in her TED Talk[7] how men and women manage shame differently, what the antidote to shame is, and finishes by sharing the components of living whole-heartedly.

How Women and Men Manage Shame

Women	Men
Nice – People pleasing	Emotional control
Focus on being thin	Work comes first
Focus on outside appearances	Pursue status
Modest	Violence

For both men and women, shame is a fear of connection. Our fear of being unworthy of connection keeps us out of connection with God and people. Shame can keep us from receiving grace, mercy, and redemption. It hinders us from relating to the Holy Spirit.

Bullies and Shame: Clinical psychologist Mary C. Lamia explains in *Psychology Today* that bullies are particularly shame prone. She writes, *That means they are afraid their failures or shortcomings will be*

---

[7] Brown, B. (2014, March 11). *Listening to Shame* [Video file]. Retrieved from www.ted.com/talks/brene_brown_listening_to_shame?

exposed. A person can have problems with shame and still have high self-esteem, and this is what makes a person act like a bully. [8]

Be Courageous, Be Vulnerable

Shame needs secrecy, silence, and judgment to grow, and often manifests as blame to discharge pain and discomfort.

The antidote to shame is vulnerability. Vulnerability overcomes shame.

Vulnerability is sharing honestly and taking emotional risks with "safe people." It takes courage and practice to be vulnerable. Truth and courage aren't always comfortable, but they are true signs of strength, not weakness. So often we try to look perfect to everyone to impress them and earn their love. We don't want to let them know about our weaknesses or failures. This is the opposite of vulnerability.

As we allow ourselves to be seen, connection becomes possible. Connecting with safe people often brings a sense of love and belonging, which helps us grow in intimacy with God and others. In our healing from shame, we begin to believe that we are loved and belong in God's family (even if we make mistakes and lack perfection). We start to believe we're "enough." The Gratitude and Appreciation Exercises from Step Two can help you stay relationally connected as you practice vulnerability with others.

To be Healthy and Whole-hearted

- Allow yourself to be imperfect and tell the story of who you are.
- Have compassion for yourself - without it for yourself, you cannot have it for others.
- Embrace vulnerability – believe that vulnerability makes you beautiful.
- Be willing to invest in relationships that may not work out and love people even when there are no guarantees.
- Vulnerability is letting go of control and being able to predict the outcome.
- As you allow yourself the courage to be imperfect, you'll start letting go of who you think you should be in order to be who you are.
- Be creative and loving and trust that "I am enough."
- Be kind and gentle with yourself, for then you'll be kinder and gentler to everyone else.

---

[8] Lamia, M.C. (2010, October 22). *Do Bullies Really Have Low Self-esteem?* Retrieved from www.psychologytoday.com/blog/intense-emotions-and-strong-feelings/201010/do-bullies-really-have-low-self-esteem

Love Bonds Versus Fear Bonds in Relationships

(From *Living from the Heart Jesus Gave You*[9])

LOVE BONDS	FEAR BONDS
Based on love and characterized by truth, closeness, intimacy, joy, peace, perseverance, and authentic giving.	**Based on fear** and characterized by pain, humiliation, desperation, shame, guile, and/or fear of rejection, abandonment, or other detrimental consequences.
Desire driven – I bond with you because I want to be with you.	**Avoidance driven** – I bond with you because I want to avoid negative feelings or pain.
Grow stronger both when we move closer and when we move away from each other – When we move closer, I get to know you better. When we move away from each other, I am still blessed by the memory of you.	**Grow stronger only by moving closer or by moving further away** – The closer we are, the scarier it gets, so I must avoid closeness. The further apart we are, the scarier it gets, so I need to manipulate closeness.
We can share both positive and negative feelings – The bond is strengthened by this truthful sharing.	**We cannot share both positive and negative feelings** —The bond is strengthened by (1) avoiding negative or positive feelings, or (2) by seeking only negative feelings or seeking only positive feelings.
Participants on both ends of the bond benefit—The bond encourages all people to act like themselves.	**Participants on only one end of the bond benefit**—The bond keeps people from acting like themselves.
Truth pervades the relationship.	**Deceit and pretending pervades the relationship.**
Grow and mature people—Equipping people to find their hearts.	**Restrict and stunt growth**—Keeping people from finding their hearts.
Govern "How do I act like myself?"	**Govern "How do I solve problems?"**

Love bonds are healthy relationships that are mutually beneficial to both or all participants. My prayer for you is that you will seek to develop healthy, life-giving, love bonds in all your relationships. Where you find fear, exchange it for love.

It's not easy, but it's worth it—you're worth it.

For God has not given us a spirit of fear and timidity, but of power, love, and self-discipline.
2 Timothy 1:7 (NLT)

---

[9] Wilder, E.J., Friesen, J., Bierling, A.M., Koepcke, R., Poole, M. *Living From The Heart Jesus Gave You* (2013). Shepherd's House Inc. Used with permission.

Step Five
Homework & Journaling

Step Five: I will identify areas where I need to take responsibility.

The person who abused me is responsible for the abusive acts committed against me. I will not accept the guilt and shame resulting from those acts.

1. What have I been told I'm responsible for concerning the abuse in my life?

2. Which messages have I or do I continue to accept as truth?

3. What behaviors or choices have I felt bad or sad about?

4. In what areas do I see myself as defective or imperfect?

5. How can I practice being vulnerable with the safe people in my life? (Examples: Sharing parts of my story, being open about my feelings, asking people to pray for my needs, finding a mentor or prayer partner to support you in your journey.)

6. Does the idea of connection in relationships cause me to experience fear and anxiety? Can I identify <u>what</u> I'm afraid of? What is it?

7. I would like to ask God to help me overcome some areas in my life where I am wanting more freedom. Holy Spirit, help me learn how to trust you more for:

8. What are my biggest "take aways" from this lesson? What are the key things that will help me to let go of false responsibility and start seeing myself the way God sees me?

Possible Prayer:

Father, am I believing something about myself that isn't true? (write down what lie about yourself God is revealing) _____

Am I believing something about You that isn't true? (write down what lie about God that He is revealing to you) _____

Father forgive me for believing the lie that _____, I choose today to reject that lie. I renounce it, in Jesus name, and I command it to leave me now. I pray Father that You would heal my mind, my heart, and my body, from all the effects of that lie and restore what the enemy has taken from me. As I give You my hurt, my pain, and my disappointment, I surrender that lie to You.

What truth do You want to give me in its place? (write down what truth God is revealing to you)

_____

Step Six: Share My Feelings with Others

Step Six: I will practice trusting others by sharing my feelings, including anger, fear, sadness, and joy.

Isaiah 53:3 *He was despised and rejected by men; a man of sorrows and familiar with suffering.*

John 11:35 *Jesus wept.*

Many times, we hear people talking about feelings in a negative context:

> "Feelings aren't important." "Emotions get in the way."
> "Don't trust your feelings." "Don't feel sad." "Just trust God."

Have you heard advice like this?

What does the Bible say?

The Bible describes more than 20 emotions that Jesus felt. And they weren't all happy feelings either! Jesus felt affection, anguish, anger, compassion, distress, grief, gladness, indignation, joy, love, peace, sadness, sympathy, uneasiness, and weariness.

Jesus allowed Himself to fully feel the entire spectrum of human emotions. As your model for spiritual and emotional maturity, He gives you the grace and the permission to fully feel your emotions as well.

Expressing Your Feelings

We either talk them out, act them out or leak them out.
– Peter Scazzero, author of *Emotionally Healthy Relationships*

Expressing and honoring your feelings isn't about being self-absorbed, arrogant, or better than anyone – it's about being true to yourself, honest with how you feel and what you need.

By not honoring your feelings, you discount yourself in painful, and damaging ways, and you create separation between yourself and others (usually the most important people in your life).

You may have learned to label your emotions as "good" or "bad." However, all emotions are God-given and can be handled in a Godly way. When you suppress pain and "bad" feelings, your brain also represses joy and "good" feelings. Your brain does not have the capacity to suppress only one emotion, such as pain or anger. When one emotion is shut down, all your emotions are shut down.

How did I feel today?

Use the list of emotions to describe how you felt today. You can use as many emotions as your like.

Happy
Calm
Cheerful
Confident
Content
Delighted
Excited
Glad
Loved
Proud
Relaxed
Satisfied
Silly
Terrific
Thankful

Sad
Ashamed
Awful
Disappointed
Discouraged
Gloomy
Hurt
Lonely
Miserable
Sorry
Unhappy
Unloved
Withdrawn

Angry
Annoyed
Bugged
Destructive
Disgusted
Frustrated
Fuming
Furious
Grumpy
Irritated
Mad
Mean
Violent

Other feelings
Afraid
Anxious
Ashamed
Bored
Confused
Curious
Embarrassed
Jealous
Moody
Responsible
Scared
Shy
Uncomfortable
Worried

	Morning	Afternoon	Evening
Monday			
Tuesday			
Wednesday			
Thursday			
Friday			
Saturday			
Sunday			

www.RewardCharts4Kids.com

DISCUSS: For our time of "check-in" today share something about your week and then share what kind of feelings you are experiencing from that situation. (If you are ready to do so - it is ok to "pass" if you do not want to share.)

Suppressed Emotions

Emotions control your thinking, your behavior, and your actions. They affect your physical body, both positively and negatively. When you ignore, dismiss, repress, or only vent your emotions, they are not properly felt and can cause serious physical illness.

Negative emotions like fear, anxiety, negativity, frustration, and depression cause chemical reactions in your body that are very different from the chemicals released when we feel positive emotions.

The four tanks of self:

When you have unresolved issues, all four of tanks of your whole person are affected.

- Mind: your conscious thinking and reasoning.
- Body: your physical part, including nerves, senses, organs, brain, cells.
- Spirit: your connection to God and others.
- Soul: your beliefs, emotions, and memories.

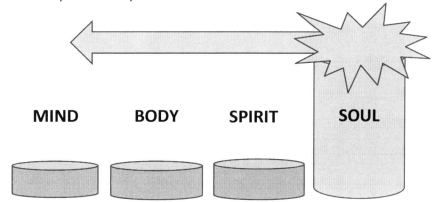

When your emotions (soul tank) are repressed or inappropriately overflowing, your **spirit tank** is affected, making it harder to hear Jesus, connect with Him on a deep level, and trust Him. Your **mind tank** is also affected, causing you confusion and an inability to think clearly and make decisions. Your **body tank**, overwhelmed with carrying all the unresolved emotions, makes you feel exhausted and depressed.

When you begin, with God's help, to process your unresolved emotions, the tanks begin to even out and your body, spirit, and mind gain clarity and strength.

There are many signs of unresolved emotions, including:

- A rawness and hurt that doesn't go away.
- Negative feelings rising often to the surface.
- You are overly sensitive to events in your past.
- Irritability, lashing out, inappropriate anger.
- Low tolerance of others.
- Critical and judgmental.
- Hard time forgiving yourself and others.
- Feeling angry towards God.
- Self-hatred.
- Escapism, including fantasy and all forms of addiction.
- Self-harm behaviors.
- Perfectionism, overly driven.
- Feelings of hopelessness.

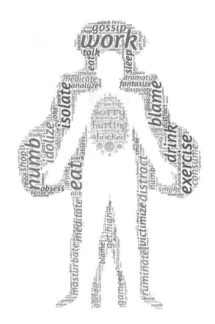

God invites you to bring Him these emotions now so He can heal them and replace them with His love and His truth.

As you begin to identify unresolved feelings, you may feel as if taking the risk to trust someone with your emotions is too challenging. This may be especially true if your trust has been broken. However, with God's help, you CAN move past the heartbreak of broken trust. Even if you've been deeply wounded or experienced traumatic and repeated episodes of betrayal, you don't have to let another person's untrustworthiness affect your ability to trust again.

Step Six
Homework & Journaling

Step Six: I will practice trusting others by sharing my feelings, including anger, fear, sadness, and joy.
Samuel 1:9-18, Isaiah 53:3

1. How were feelings expressed (or not expressed) in my childhood years? Did I feel safe to share my feelings with my family and/or friends?

2. Do I feel comfortable with emotional expression as an adult? What are my normal responses when I feel overwhelmed with feelings that are not comfortable?

3. Refer to the Joy Illustration on page 28 in Step Two. Do I know how to return to Joy when I am feeling one of the "big six emotions"? Which ones are the most difficult for me?

4. The method is not important but expressing your feelings is critical to your healing process.

   To express your feelings of anger, fear, anxiety, sadness, or grief regarding an event or events of abuse in your life, use the space below for one or more of the following methods: drawing, art, poetry, letter writing, journaling, descriptive writing…

Step Seven: Forgiveness

Step Seven: I will learn to forgive myself, God, and others, and let go of self-destructive behaviors that have held me captive.

Ephesians 4:32 *Be kind and compassionate to one another, forgiving each other, just as in Christ God forgave you.*

Matthew 6:12 *And forgive us our debts as we also have forgiven our debtors.*

Luke 23:34 *Father, forgive them for they do not know what they are doing.* (these are the words of Jesus on the cross)

Unforgiveness

Unforgiveness stems from the soul tank (emotions, memories, beliefs) we studied in the last lesson. It often leads to depression, bitterness, negativity, and almost always hurts those around you. Like suppressed and inappropriately expressed emotions, it adversely affects your body, mind, and spirit. Unforgiveness is like a wound that infects every part of you.

What forgiveness is and is not

Many of us may have a lot of misinformation about what forgiveness is and what it is not. Let's see what God says about forgiveness.

Forgiveness is not:	Forgiveness is:
Condoning the behavior – pretending something awful didn't happen.	A choice – a decision of the will.
A feeling.	A command from God, given because Jesus forgives you.
Letting the person off the hook.	Giving up your right for revenge and letting God judge their behavior.
Expecting an apology.	Agreeing to take the responsibility for your own healing from sins committed against you.
Forgetting.	A path of remembering that leads you to freedom and healing.
Necessarily letting the perpetrator back into your life or putting yourself back in danger.	Frees you up to hear God and develop healthy boundaries.

Forgiveness will bring you healing, loss of resentment and anger, and the freedom to move on. Once you forgive, you find the situation no longer has power over you.

Forgiveness is a choice

Forgiveness is a choice, a decision of your will. God commands you to forgive because Jesus forgave you, and He wants you to be free from your past.

Forgiveness is letting God do the judging.

Romans 12:19 says do not take revenge, but let God deal with the one who has hurt you.

Forgiveness is facing the consequences of their sin

Another important part of forgiveness is agreeing to face the consequences of another's sin. Here's an example: If you are run over by a drunk driver and have both of your legs broken, it's still up to you to cooperate with the doctors, to feel the pain, and to do the therapy so you can be healed.

Forgiveness is a path of remembering, a path that leads to healing and freedom

You will still remember, but as you choose to forgive and press into God's amazing healing power, the sting will dissipate, and eventually disappear.

As you forgive, the power of the offender over your life is released. When you cling to unforgiveness, you are still tied to the offender in an ungodly way. When you decide to live confined and imprisoned by what has happened to you, you are trapped. To forgive brings freedom from what was done to you.

Forgiveness and reconciliation

Forgiveness does not necessarily mean reconciliation.

Reconciliation involves two people being willing to accept responsibility for their behavior, ask forgiveness from the person they harmed and from God, as well as a willingness to let God change their behaviors into ones that are pleasing to Him.

Repentance: Matthew 3:8 says we are to produce fruit in keeping with repentance. Time will show if someone is truly repentant and wants God to change their heart. Temporary regret and true repentance are two very different things. Temporary regret usually means a person is sorry for getting caught. True repentance shows itself through changed behavior.

Forgiving God

What if you are angry or disappointed with God? Maybe you feel that God let you down or did not come through for you the way you wanted. Maybe the abuse or trauma left you feeling unprotected and wondering if your Heavenly Father really loves you or cares about what happens to you. "Why would He allow this?" Why didn't He protect me or the one I love, the way I wanted Him to?

The sense of betrayal or abandonment may leave you with unanswered questions that can lead to confusion about God's goodness or power to intervene.

It can be very helpful to read and focus on this scripture:

> **Isaiah 55:8-9** *"For My thoughts are not your thoughts, nor are your ways My ways," declares the* L<small>ORD</small>. *"For as the heavens are higher than the earth, so are My ways higher than your ways and My thoughts than your thoughts."*

Possible Prayer

> "Dear Lord, I confess that even though I know You are loving and have never done anything wrong, I have held judgments against you in my heart. I choose to release and repent from every wrong judgment and angry thought toward You. I ask You to forgive me, cleanse me and replace any lies I have believed about You with the truth."

It doesn't feel very safe to admit that you're angry with God, but He knows what's in your heart. Alternatively, hiding your feelings gives the enemy an advantage and builds a wall between you and God.

When you choose to face your feelings toward God and acknowledge that He is sovereign and His ways are not yours, it brings freedom.

Divine Exchange

At this point you may want to ask God for a Divine Exchange:

> "Dear Lord, I hand to you my anger, disappointment, and pain. What do You have for me in exchange?" (explanation follows)

God is a God of exchange: The Word says that He gives you eternal life instead of death. Revelation 21:4 says,

> *He will wipe away every tear from their eyes. There will be no more death or mourning or crying or pain, for the old order of things has passed away.*

What exciting promises! Once you give your life to the Lord, you will have eternal life with Him instead of eternal separation and death.

God does not just wait until we leave this earth to give us His divine exchanges. For example, Isaiah 61:5 tells us that He gives you a crown of beauty for ashes, the oil of gladness for mourning, a garment of praise for a spirit of despair.

He invites you to come to Him with your pain and sorrow and He is right there, ready to give you His wonderful replacements.

You can give the negative things you've been carrying to the Lord knowing He has great and wonderful things for them in exchange. Examples of things you can give Him besides unforgiveness: shame, false responsibility, fear, anger, and revenge.

Forgiving Yourself

You may also need to forgive yourself.

Have you made poor choices? Even though your poor choices may have been influenced by your victimization, it does not justify behavior that goes against God's will.

As you ask for forgiveness, He cleanses you, and He remembers it no more. Forgiving yourself involves seeing yourself the way God sees you. His love will heal you and help you to grow into the person He created you to be.

Regardless of what you've done in your past, whether it be an abortion, fornication, or some other embarrassing sin, it's vital that you forgive yourself from everything in your past that you are ashamed of. If God chose to forget your sins for His sake, then you ought to do the same.

Isaiah 43:25, *I, even I, am he that blots out your transgressions for my own sake, and remembers your sin no more.*

Psalms 103:12, *As far as the east is from the west, so far hath he removed our transgressions from us.*

God's Word says that He has completely removed your sins from you! If you continually beat up on yourself, you're practicing false guilt, which is a tool the enemy uses to pull you down.

When you continue to associate yourself with your sinful past, then you need to change the way you see things... why? **Because the way you are thinking does not line up with what God's Word says.**

When you associate yourself with your past failures, after God's Word has assured you that they have been removed from you, do you realize you're not believing what God's Word is saying to you?

Choose to forgive yourself, and then align your thinking with what God says in His Word.

God says it's removed from you. Take Him at His Word and believe Him!

Step Seven
Homework & Journaling

Step Seven: I will learn to forgive myself, God, and others, and let go of self-destructive behaviors that have held me captive.
Matthew 6:12, Ephesians 4:32

1. How would I define forgiveness? What does it mean to me?

2. What part do I feel forgiveness plays in my healing process?

3. What have I been taught about forgiving those who have offended or hurt me?

4. Write a letter to God expressing current adult feelings and/or struggles with forgiveness.

5. What would God write back to me?

6. What is the most challenging part of this step for you?

    - Forgiving others.
    - Letting go of disappoint/anger towards God.
    - Forgiving yourself and letting go of shame.

Step Eight: Developing Healthy Relationships

Step Eight: I will develop positive relationships with God and others by learning appropriate boundaries and the skills necessary for healthy relationships.

I will take steps to continue my healing by changing unhealthy behaviors, growing in relationships, and developing a positive support system in my church and in my community.

John 15:9, 17 *As the Father has loved me, so have I loved you. Now remain in my love.*

Psalm 16:6 *The boundary lines have fallen for me in pleasant places; surely, I have a delightful inheritance.*

Psalm 74:16-17 *The day is yours, and yours also the night; you established the sun and moon. It was you who set all the boundaries of the earth; you made both summer and winter.*

II Corinthians 5:17 *Therefore, if anyone is in Christ, the new creation has come: The old has gone, the new is here!*

Ecclesiastes 4:9-10 *Two are better than one, because they have a good return for their labor: If either of them falls down, one can help the other up. But pity anyone who falls and has no one to help them up.*

Created for Relationship

Whether or not you realize it, God created you for relationship. Some of your relationships are fleeting—a few words spoken with the check-out clerk, the neighbor you wave to as the garage door closes behind you, etc. You also have acquaintances—people you may interact with frequently, but not in great depth—co-workers, people at church, the neighbor whose name you do not remember.

You may also have intimate, trusting relationships. A person or a few people who you're completely honest with, who you're completely yourself with. A person or people you trust with your heart. God created you in His image, so He could have this kind of relationship with you.

In Genesis, we read that God had an intimate and trusting relationship with Adam and Eve until the enemy of their soul led the two into sin. Darn that serpent! Relationships haven't been the same since Adam and Eve took the advice of the serpent and ate the fruit of the tree God forbid them to eat from. Ever since, relationships have been difficult.

Three Types of Relationships

There are three primary types of relationships: the controlling relationship, the separated relationship, and the healthy relationship.

Controlling Relationship: You must conform and surrender to my wishes

In a controlling relationship, one person has all the power.

An abusive relationship is an excellent example of a controlling relationship.

Fear and insecurity: The reasons people become controlling in a relationship are often the same reasons that people allow themselves to be controlled in a relationship—insecurity, fear, and family of origin.

Fear and insecurity are powerful emotions that can lead to devastating choices.

Family of origin: We are all products of our childhood environment. If you grow up seeing your daddy abuse your mommy, unless someone intervenes to teach you otherwise, you may assume the behavior is normal, leading you to behave the same way as an adult.

When a child feels as though they have no control over their own life, they may continue that powerlessness pattern, or rebel against it by becoming controlling to compensate for the lack of control they felt in childhood.

In a controlling relationship no one is happy, no one is satisfied. Without intervention, both parties continue a downward spiral toward self-destruction—emotionally, and sometimes physically, sexually, and spiritually.

Some people are so determined to avoid a controlling relationship that they're caught in another relationship trap...

Separated Relationship: You stay over there. I'll stay over here.

The separated relationship is another example of an unhealthy relationship. This is a relationship of self-protection. If no one gets close, I don't get hurt.

The problem with this is that while pain, loss, and disappointment are being kept out, so are joy, love, and connection.

God never meant for us to live alone and isolated. That's why He created Eve. Because He knew that, *It is not good for man to be alone.* (Genesis 2:18) The same goes for women.

This disconnected lifestyle leads to loneliness, fear, and emotional and physical deterioration.

Healthy Relationship

God created us because He wants to be in relationship with us. If God sees the value in relationship, it just might be worth the risk to reach out to others, to allow them to draw near; to risk knowing and being known; to risk being hurt, maybe even rejected occasionally, so we can delight in the benefits of joy, love, and connection with God and His other children.

As we make those connections, our goal is to develop healthy relationships where each party has equal power and value, relationships where we are each still ourselves while sharing ourselves with one other. We allow others to enter our lives and we are welcomed into theirs.

In the Gospel of John, Jesus says He is in us and we are in Him. If it's good enough for Jesus, who are we to argue?

In a healthy relationship, both or all parties contribute.

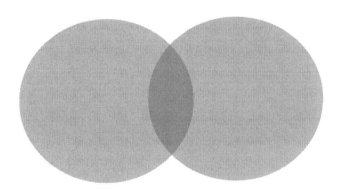

Healthy Relationship:

Equal size, power, value, and defined sharing of each other

Healthy relationships are not just for couples: besides couples, healthy relationships are for families, friends, churches, and communities. We each bring our knowledge, insight, experiences, and fun to the party. We each bring needed support, compassion, healing, and power. We each give and we each receive. I color your world and you color mine.

Healthy relationships are not always easy: In healthy relationships, we are able to speak truth into another's life and they are welcome to speak truth into ours. We won't always agree. Participation in a healthy relationship doesn't mean being and thinking and believing the same way about all things. **It means loving, accepting, and respecting the other person and their right to have a different viewpoint**.

Boundaries

An important key to a healthy relationship is healthy boundaries.

Physical boundaries are all around us. Boundaries keep us safe. Boundaries provide definition. Our skin is a type of boundary. It shows where my body ends, and another's begins. Hold your hand up to the person next to you or, if you are alone, hold your hands with palms facing up. The two hands do not merge. They are separate entities.

The fence around a yard is a boundary. It defines what's my yard and what's my neighbor's yard. My yard is my responsibility. It's up to me to water my grass, mow my lawn, and plant my flowers. I decide who comes into my yard. My neighbor's yard is her responsibility. She chooses what she'll have in her garden, the kind of trees she'll have and who can enter her yard.

My Yard - Your Yard

Yard Illustration: We choose what we want to put in our "yard." It is our responsibility. What happens in our neighbor's "yard" is their responsibility. You shouldn't plant flowers in your neighbor's yard without their permission or against their will. And they shouldn't come and pull out your flowers, even if they think your yard is full of weeds. The yard represents your life. You are responsible for your own feelings, attitudes and behaviors, and your neighbor is responsible for theirs.

We all have a special garden we are called to plant, tend, and protect. This garden is our life. Your "yard" is you. It is who you are, who God has made you to be. Often, you may have no idea who that is. Maybe you've allowed the world to define you. Maybe you've left the gates of your life open to others and allowed them to trample your yard.

Personal Boundaries

There are some boundaries that are more important than physical boundaries: personal boundaries. Personal boundaries define your personal space - where you end, and others begin. They help you understand your personal identity and help you maintain that identity.

Psalm 74 talks about some of the physical boundaries God has set in place. Scripture also reveals the personal boundaries God has set. He is God, we are not. He tells us in His Word what He will and will not allow, what He likes and what He doesn't like. **God's boundaries provide safety and security for His children.** We don't have to guess or wonder whether the choices we make please Him. We can know what pleases Him. We can know what He allows.

"Sea Roses With Fence" (CC BY 2.0) by Me in ME. flickr.com/photos/pavdw/35068353564/

The people around you deserve no less. You have a responsibility, not only to yourself, but to those around you to set reasonable personal boundaries. Setting boundaries is not selfish. Setting boundaries is not restrictive. Setting boundaries is generous and freeing.

Personal boundaries provide a safe place to discover who God made you to be. They are not a rock wall (keeping everyone out) but are like a good fence with a wide gate. That gate, though, only has a latch on the inside. You alone decide who and what comes in, and who and what goes out. Through your gate, you welcome in people and circumstances that nurture your life. Through your gate, you release pain, sin, fear, bitterness - anything that prevents you from becoming all God created you to be.

Boundaries help you to discover and communicate to others what you will and will not allow in your life. Others don't have to agree with your boundaries.

An important aspect of personal boundaries is allowing others to set their boundaries, as well. You are responsible for your boundaries; they are responsible for theirs, or lack thereof, as well as the resulting consequences. Your boundaries free you from taking on responsibilities, feelings, and consequences that don't belong to you.

If you have lived a long time without boundaries it will take time, dedication, and patience to build your fence and your gates. It's journey of discovery and change. Change may be difficult for you and for those around you. It's important to use wisdom on this journey, so you know when, where, and with whom it's safe to set new boundaries.

In severely abusive, violent situations, setting new boundaries must be approached with great caution, so you do not place yourself in more danger. This is one reason why a good support system is so important in creating new boundaries.

You need support: As you begin your journey of discovery and creating boundaries, surround yourself with safe, Godly people, who will walk with you. This support group is one example of a safe and supportive place. This journey will take time. Be patient and gentle with yourself and with others. We're all learning something new and it won't be easy, but it will be worth it.

Types of Boundaries

Living with healthy boundaries begins by identifying boundaries. This list of boundaries will help you get started with identifying your own boundaries and what you might need to work on.

Skin
- Skin on your body.
- Touch – abuse – etc.

Word
- Especially the word **no.**
- What are some other words we can use to set boundaries?

Truth
- Truth about God.
- Truth about ourselves – who we are.
- Overcoming lies about God's Character.
- Overcoming lies that others have spoken over us.
- Overcoming lies we believe about ourselves.

Time
- Time away from someone or something can be healthy.
- Examples? From people, work situations, other obligations.
- Taking a break – a vacation – a prayer retreat.

Geographical Distance
- It may be necessary to completely remove yourself from a situation.
- Relationship, work, bad situations.

Emotional Distance
- Guard your heart – how much will you trust this person?
- How much will you open and share your story with this person?
- How much will you let someone else "dump" their problems on you?

Other People: Support Group
- Find people who understand boundaries and can help you set and keep them. Being in a support group during this time can give you the support you need to stay firm.
- Accountability Partner.

Consequences:
- Setting and enforcing consequences will show people that you are serious about keeping your boundaries. You are choosing to not participate in another person's negative behavior. If it is safe to do so, try to communicate ahead of time what the consequences will be if they violate your boundaries.
- It's ok to have consequences. Recognize that consequences are a result of choices they've made to engage in unhealthy behaviors or actions.

Godly Boundaries

GOD APPROVES OF BOUNDARIES
Boundaries are a natural part of creation. The sea only comes so far, the hills only climb so high, the sky stops where it meets the ground. God, Himself, shows us the perfect example of personal boundary-setting. He defines who He is...He is God, we are not. He tells us in His Word what He will and will not allow, what He likes and what He does not like. God's boundaries provide safety and security for His creation.

PERSONAL BOUNDARIES
Define what is me and what is not me; where I end, and where others begin. Personal boundaries help me understand what I am responsible for and set me free from taking on responsibilities, feelings, and consequences that do not belong to me.

BOUNDARIES HELP KEEP THE GOOD IN AND THE BAD OUT
Boundaries are not walls. Our boundaries need to have gates. Through our gates we welcome in people and circumstances that nurture who we are. Through our gates we release pain, sin, fear—anything that violates our boundaries and prevents us from becoming all that God created us to be.

BOUNDARIES SET US FREE TO LOVE
Good boundaries provide the security we need to reach out to others in love. Good boundaries free us from the need to judge or control others. We allow them to reap what they sow—to the good or to the bad. Having boundaries that are clearly understood (by us) and communicated (to others) frees us to be ourselves and to allow others to be themselves.

I Will Take Steps

"I will take steps" says more than "I will *try* to take steps." *Try* leaves room for failure. How often do you say you will *try*, when you really mean, "I probably won't do this, but don't want to admit that, so I'll pretend

> *A commitment to God is a commitment harder to ignore than any other.*
>
> *Years ago, there was a diet book going around the Christian community. I bought the book but couldn't start the diet. The first principle was to make a promise to God about my eating habits and food choices. I knew I wasn't ready to make that commitment, so I set the book aside.*
>
> *I hope you're ready to make the commitment to God to take the steps necessary to continue your healing. I know He's ready to commit to walk alongside you every step of the way.*
>
> Diane Stores, Door of Hope Founder

I'm going to do this?"

Saying, "I will take steps" is making a commitment. Who are you making this commitment to? To yourself? Good. To your family? Also, good. To God? Better...Best.

Given your whole life to Christ yet?

Have you given your whole life to Christ yet? Over your lifetime, you may have given away bits and pieces of yourself to people and organizations which have abused and misused you.

Jesus will never use or abuse you. He also will not settle for bits and pieces of you. He wants all of you. He wants your beautiful parts. He wants the ugly parts you try to hide. He wants your weaknesses and your strengths. He wants your mind, heart, and body. He wants it all, because it is all precious to Him. You are precious to Him. Of all the relationships you will have in this life, the relationship you have with Jesus is the most important. He is the One who will never leave you nor forsake you (Deuteronomy 31:8).

You can come to Jesus with your sin, your selfishness, your mistakes, your confusion, your unbelief, and He'll take it all. He stands with arms outstretched to bring you close, to fill you with the peace and love you've been searching for all your life.

Jesus is the right place. Jesus has more love than you can hope for or imagine. He's not waiting for you to clean up before coming. He just wants you to come. He's drawn the bath. He'll take the responsibility for cleaning up anything that needs cleaning. He just wants to love on you, to comfort you, to heal you. If you have never invited Jesus into your life, or even if you have, but want to recommit to your relationship with the Lord, take a minute to pray the following prayer - or one with your own words.

"Jesus, I confess that I have been willful. I have made choices that have been destructive to myself and to others. I have ignored your invitation to be part of a greater family, to be Your child and receive Your love. I confess that I do not understand how You could love me or why You would want me to draw near to You. But, Jesus, I choose to lay my doubts aside. I choose to believe that you are who You say You are and that I am who You say I am. Today, I choose You. Today, I choose to become a new creation."

If you have chosen to pray that prayer, to give your whole life to Christ, welcome to the family! You are no longer alone.

Please tell someone in the group about your decision to follow Christ. Life is a challenging journey and learning to follow Jesus is best done with others. Besides, it's more fun that way, as we learn from and encourage one another.

Changing Unhealthy Patterns

Regret: Regret after apologizing and making amends is unhealthy. We've all made mistakes. We've all made choices that haven't worked well. We've spoken up when we should have kept silent. We've kept silent when we should have spoken, acted when we should have waited; waited when we should have acted. We don't get through life without making mistakes. Admit them, apologize for them, and make amends. Then move on. God has forgiven you.

Who authors your life? Have you spent too much of your life allowing, or even inviting, others to define who you are and to direct your steps?

Hebrews 12:1-2

God is your creator. He created you with specific intent, with a specific purpose. Tune your ears away from the world and toward the Lord. Only He has the right and ability to reveal who He created you to be and how to live out your divine destiny. You can trust Him to gently make known any areas you need to change, and He will give you the tools, strength, and courage to make those changes.

Start with Jesus

Growing in relationships can be difficult. We've looked at some of the differences between healthy and unhealthy relationships. We've begun to understand the importance of boundaries in relationships. Now, it's time to put what you've learned into practice. A great place to start is your relationship with Jesus. There is no one safer than Jesus. You can be yourself with Him without fear that He will leave you, mock you, or talk about you behind your back.

As you build your relationship with Him, He will help you feel more confident to reach out to others. He will help you recognize who's safe to let through your gates and who's not.

Go Slow

It is important that you move slowly into new relationships. Take time to let others earn your trust. A relationship is giving and taking—a two-way interaction. Any relationship that's all one way or the other is not a relationship.

Develop a positive support system in the church and the community

This is an easy one! By being in this group, you've already begun.

Hopefully, this group has been a positive support system for you and that you've learned how to receive and give support in a healthy manner.

The safety of a support group gives you strength to tell the truth about how things really are and how to do so without damaging others. It reminds you that you're not alone and supports you to understand it's ok to say no to others and yes to yourself.

Take what you've learned, and the great love Jesus has for you, and do two things:

1. Nurture them and help them grow
2. Share them with others

The closure of this group is not the end. It's the beginning. Consider repeating this group and/or attending another Door of Hope support group to continue your healing journey and to continue to build your "support team."

It's time for you to take your new tools and start building a new life with new memories.

Other Resources and Groups

Additional resources are listed on page 85 and at doorofhopeministries.org/resources

To find a Door of Hope support group in your area or one you can attend online, visit doorofhopeministries.org/events.

To not miss any Door of Hope offerings, join our e-news at doorofhopministries.org/newsletter

Step Eight
Homework & Journaling

Step Eight: I will develop positive relationships with God and others by learning appropriate boundaries and the skills necessary for healthy relationships.

I will take steps to continue my healing by changing unhealthy behaviors, growing in relationships, and developing a positive support system in my church and in my community.

1. In which of my relationships do I take...

    a) a passive role?

    b) an aggressive role?

    c) a passive-aggressive role?

    d) an assertive role?

2. Are there areas in my life where I have good boundaries? Explain.

3. Are there areas in my life where I need to work on having healthy boundaries? Explain.

4. Do you ever say "Yes" when you really want to say "No"? In what kinds of situations does that happen most often?

5. How do you respond to others when they say "No"? Is it hard for you? Does it feel like rejection?

6. How would I describe my relationship with God? Does God allow me to set boundaries with Him? Does He set boundaries with me?

7. How have I experienced positive support from my *Healing from Abuse: Authentic Hope Support Group?* What kind of support do I need to continue my healing process?

Recommended Resources

brenebrown.com - Brené Brown, a word-renowned speaker and best-selling author, is a research professor in Texas studying vulnerability, courage, authenticity and shame. Her website offers materials for purchase as well as free downloads, articles and more.

deeperwalkinternational.org - Deeper Walk International equips individuals and helps the church develop spiritually minded, emotionally mature, relationally connected followers of Jesus. Their model can be applied to discipleship, leadership, student ministry, marriage, family and more. This website offers free resources, including eight sessions of a free online course. You'll also find books and online courses for purchase.

focusministries1.org – FOCUS Ministries is a nonprofit organization offering support, education, spiritual direction, and assistance to teens, women, and families in the Chicago area experiencing domestic violence, destructive relationships, separation, or divorce. This website has books for sale and free resources for women, teens, pastors, and more.

immanuelapproach.com - The Immanuel Approach describes a faith-based (Christian) approach to healing for emotional trauma, and then applies the same principles and techniques for building an "Immanuel lifestyle." This website provides resources for anyone wanting to learn about, receive, facilitate, or teach the Immanuel Approach.

drleaf.com - Dr. Caroline Leaf is a cognitive neuroscientist specializing in cognitive and metacognitive neuropsychology. Her passion is to help people see the power of the mind and the link between science and God so they can control their thoughts and emotions and learn how to find their purpose. In addition to her online store, her website has free videos, downloads, blog posts, and links to her podcast.

leslievernick.com – Leslie Vernick is an experienced Christ-centered counselor, coach and author of seven books, including the national bestseller, *The Emotionally Destructive Relationship*. Her website has free and for-purchase resources for those desiring healing, and for who minister to them.

lifemodelworks.org – Life Model Works links brain science with the Bible to create simple, practical tools for churches to build authentic community and help transform lives. On this website you can buy books and subscribe to receive a growing library of resources. You'll also find free resources for individuals and small groups, including an app to help you find peace.

nicabm.com - The National Institute for the Clinical Application of Behavioral Medicine (NICABM) is at the forefront of developing and delivering programs with "take home" ideas immediately adaptable for practitioners to use with their patients. Their website offers accredited advanced learning courses for practitioners and has links to their free blog and videos related to trauma, mindfulness, the brain, and the mind/body connection.

Healing from Abuse:
Authentic Hope Support Group
Evaluation Form

1. What is your overall impression of the *Healing from Abuse: Authentic Hope Support Group*?

_____
_____
_____
_____

2. How was the group most helpful in your healing process?

_____
_____
_____
_____

3. Was there anything you hoped to receive through this group that you did not?

_____
_____
_____
_____

4. Comments regarding the length of the group.

_____

_____

5. Please evaluate the group's leadership.

_____

_____

_____

_____

6. Please give us your overall impression of the group manual.

_____

_____

_____

_____

7. Would you recommend this group to another woman? _____ Yes _____ No

8. Are there any churches you believe would be interested in hosting a *Healing from Abuse: Authentic Hope Support Group*? If so, which one?
_____

9. Would you be interested in attending another group? _____ Yes _____ No

10. Would you allow us to use your testimony in our newsletter: _____ Yes _____ No

11. Any other feedback?

_____

_____

_____

_____

Made in the USA
Middletown, DE
03 June 2023

31887999R10051